# KEYNES AND LAISSEZ-FAIRE

*Also by A. P. Thirlwall*

GROWTH AND DEVELOPMENT WITH SPECIAL REFERENCE TO DEVELOPING ECONOMIES
INFLATION, SAVING AND GROWTH IN DEVELOPING ECONOMIES
REGIONAL GROWTH AND UNEMPLOYMENT IN THE UNITED KINGDOM (*with R. J. Dixon*)
FINANCING ECONOMIC DEVELOPMENT
KEYNES AND INTERNATIONAL MONETARY RELATIONS (*ed.*)

# KEYNES AND LAISSEZ-FAIRE

## *The Third Keynes Seminar held at the University of Kent at Canterbury 1976*

*edited by*

A.P. THIRLWALL

*Professor of Applied Economics*
*University of Kent at Canterbury*



M

*First published 1978 by*
THE MACMILLAN PRESS LTD
*London and Basingstoke*
*Associated companies in Delhi*
*Dublin Hong Kong Johannesburg Lagos*
*Melbourne New York Singapore Tokyo*

British Library Cataloguing in Publication Data

Keynes Seminar, 3rd, University of Kent at Canterbury, 1976
Keynes and laissez-faire
1. Keynes, John Maynard, *Baron Keynes* – Congresses 2. Laissez-faire – Congresses
I. Title II. Thirlwall, Anthony Philip
III. Keynes College
330.15′3 HB95
ISBN 0-333-19878-6



*Printed in Hong Kong by*
SHANGHAI PRINTING PRESS LIMITED

*This book is sold subject*
*to the standard conditions*
*of the Net Book Agreement*

# Contents

# List of Participants

*Speakers and contributors to the discussion*

Lord Balogh *Oxford*
Sir Alec Cairncross *Oxford*
Mr L. Carr *Treasury, London*
Mr D. Crabtree *University of Kent*
Professor M. Cranston *London School of Economics*
Professor B. Corry *Queen Mary College, London*
Mr M. Daines *Queen Mary College, London*
Dr Dean *North London Polytechnic*
Professor W. Hagenbuch *University of Kent*
Mr J. Hoffman *Bank of England*
Professor T. Hutchinson *University of Birmingham*
Dr R. G. Jones *University of Kent*
Mr J. Kemp *London*
Professor C. Kennedy *University of Kent*
Dr E. Nabiel *Lancaster Polytechnic*
Mr S. Oksuz *University of Kent*
Mr R. Opie *Oxford*
Sir Austin Robinson *Cambridge*
Dr R. Skidelsky *North London Polytechnic*
Professor M. Vile *University of Kent*

# Acknowledgements

The editor wishes to thank the Royal Economic Society for the frontispiece; and Marion Beale who transcribed the tapes of the seminar and typed the final draft of the manuscript. A.P.T.

# Foreword

The first Keynes seminar was four years ago almost to the day. We already begin to feel that the seminars have a very settled existence, and it is a matter of great pleasure to welcome back to the seminar some of the people who have contributed to the success of previous occasions, in particular Lord Kahn, Sir Austin Robinson and Miss Mary Glasgow who have added to our seminars not only of their knowledge but also the aura which comes from close contact with Lord Keynes. It is also a special pleasure to welcome Mr Stephen Keynes and Dr Milo Keynes. At the initiation of these seminars Dr Milo Keynes gave much valued advice and information. He was also at the time preparing his own book *Essays on John Maynard Keynes*, and I would like to say in passing that the way in which the book demonstrates the range and depth of Lord Keynes's interests gives us every encouragement to think that our seminars have a long future ahead of them. We shall not run short of subject matter.

Perhaps at this point I could also say to a wider public, and to avoid misunderstanding among reviewers of the proceedings of these seminars, that the Keynes Seminar is not a conventional seminar comprised solely of academic (economic) specialists. It is an occasion for Keynes College, and comprises, as do colleges, junior and senior members from all disciplines. The seminars thus serve an educational as well as an academic role.

There are two very considerable grounds for regret in opening this seminar today. Professor Spence, first Master of the College, died earlier in the year and his loss is felt all the more keenly today. The idea behind the seminars, to commemorate the memory of Lord Keynes, was his. To many of us they represent in a most obvious and conspicuous way Professor Spence's contribution to the College. A lecture, it might be thought, conveys the impression of definitiveness and certainty;

a magisterial summing up and laying down of the truth. By contrast a seminar is most obviously a process of exploration, an invitation to consider differing viewpoints. It represents, one might say, a civilised disagreement. I think Professor Spence liked to think of college life in general as providing the opportunity for just such civilised disagreement. We are, however, very pleased that Mrs Spence is here with us today.

The second matter for regret is that Professor Thirlwall, who edited the proceedings of the second seminar, and who took part in the organisation of these, is prevented by illness from being with us. It is to him that we owe the theme of today's discussions. It was his happy idea to dwell on the various anniversaries which 1976 represents: 40 years since the *General Theory* was published; the bicentenary of the American Declaration of Independence, and, perhaps more important I suspect for the economist, the 200th anniversary of the publication of Adam Smith's *The Wealth of Nations*. It was Thirlwall's hope that Keynes's impact on the spirit of *laissez-faire* embodied in both documents should be explored today. The topicality of our subject needs no great underlining. At the economic level the controversy between the Keynesians and the monetarists wages fiercely, and at a deeper social and political level there is the issue as to whether overcommitment to supposedly Keynesian policies is not producing strains which really tax the survival capacity of our political institutions and social system. Lord Keynes himself would have delighted in his present controversial status. He was not himself reticent about public controversy. At the previous seminar one of the speakers observed, perhaps impishly, 'I do not think that Keynes was always right. You did know that when you invited me'. I could happily assure him that we did. If this is the measure of the stature of a thinker – that there should be searching debate and differences of opinion as to the extent and nature of his impact on his own society and the world at large – then I believe this afternoon's proceedings will show Keynes to have been a giant.

*Keynes College* D. Crabtree
*May 1977* *Master*

# Session 1

## INTRODUCTION

*Professor W. Hagenbuch* (Chairman)

This is the year of anniversaries. The Master of Keynes College has already reminded us of three: the bicentenary of the American Declaration of Independence; the 200th anniversary of the publication of Adam Smith's *Wealth of Nations*, and the 40th anniversary of the publication of the *General Theory of Employment, Interest and Money.* We can add yet another anniversary. It is exactly 50 years since Keynes published, with the Hogarth Press, his famous lecture *The End of Laissez-Faire.* It is refreshing to read that lecture again today. Let me give you two sentences from it:

> Perhaps the chief task of economists at this present hour is to distinguish afresh the agenda of government from the non-agenda; and the companion task of politics is to devise forms of government within a democracy which shall be capable of accomplishing the agenda.

and

> The most important agenda of the State relate not to those activities which private individuals are already fulfilling, but to those functions which fall outside the sphere of the individual, to those decisions which are made by no one if the State does not make them. The important thing for government is not to do things which individuals are doing already, and to do them a little better or a little worse, but to do those things which at present are not done at all.

That was written in 1926. In 1976 we are still asking what would Keynes put on the agenda today, what would he be telling us about the nature and scope and the role of economic management. In the first half of our seminar today we shall be looking at this question, first from the point of view of an historian of economic thought, and then from that of an economic adviser. We are grateful to Professor Bernard Corry for coming to give us his thoughts on the historical aspects of this question. He is Professor of Economics at Queen Mary College, London and an authority on many areas of economic thought and policy, but chiefly on the history of thought and doctrine. He is the ideal person to engage in that practice well known to theologians and recently mentioned in a review which Professor Hutchinson wrote in the *Economic History Review*: demythologising the teachings and the message of Keynes. I don't know how much demythologising he is going to do, but we are very much looking forward to hearing him. The title of his address is 'Keynes in the History of Economic Thought'.

# KEYNES IN THE HISTORY OF ECONOMIC THOUGHT: SOME REFLECTIONS

*Professor B. Corry*

I must emphasise 'some reflections' because it would be far too presumptuous to pretend that I am going to assess Keynes's place in the history of economics. Rather I shall make some comments as a sort of prologue to such a complex and complete study. My main concern here is with Keynes and the classical tradition.

Let me begin with what might be termed the popular view of Keynes's place in the development of economic ideas. Scholars may be tempted to write it off immediately as a misleading caricature, but it is more or less a story that is widely believed. It goes as follows: before Keynes's *General Theory*, apart from a minority tradition of 'cranks' who lived in the underworld of economics, the orthodox position in macroeconomics consisted of an acceptance of two interrelated propositions. They were (i) Say's Law – to be interpreted as a belief that capitalist societies were always and everywhere on their transformation frontiers, and (ii) the quantity theory of money – which meant that money was neutral in the sense that changes in its quantity had no effect on any real variables in the system.

The policy implications of this 'pre-Keynesian' view are best summarised in the infamous 'Treasury View'[1] – a view with which generations of academic economists, civil servants and finance ministers beat off any proposals for functional finance, such as deficit spending, public works and the like, suggested as means to alleviate unemployment.

The analysis in the *General Theory* destroyed both of the orthodox assumptions, and such was the speed of the revolution that barely ten years after publication the British government, for example, was able to produce the famous *White Paper on Full Employment*[2] which met with unanimous acceptance from all economists. We had all become Keynesians.

Is this a true account of what actually happened? This is what I want to discuss, not simply for the record of academic scholarship, although this should be inspiration enough. Standards of scholarship should not be at a discount even in economics! What I have to say will, I think, particularly in the later sections of the paper, be of more general interest because these issues raised are of general concern to economists and not just to 'Hopies' (Historians of Political Economy!). In order to make our task tractable I shall proceed by asking – with some attempt at answering – a series of questions. They are:

(1) What did Keynes understand by classical economics?
(2) Was he 'fair' to Pigou?
(3) What of the 'real' classical economists? Was he 'fair' to them?
(4) Macroeconomics apart, was Keynes in the 'classical' tradition?
(5) Did the Keynesian revolution need Keynes?
(6) What is the best way to change economic thinking?

We begin with Keynes's objections to, and interpretation of, classical economics. Keynes was one of those writers who laid stress on his own originality and the breaks in his own thinking with the past. In this he lines up with, for example, Adam Smith and Jevons and contrasts with, for example, J. S. Mill and Marshall – writers who were always at pains to stress the continuity of thought and reduce revolutionary elements. Of the *General Theory* Keynes writes to George Bernard Shaw:[3]

> I believe myself to be writing a book on economic theory that will largely revolutionise... the way the world thinks about economic problems. When my new theory has been duly assimilated... there will be a great change, and, in particular, the Ricardian foundations of Marxism will be knocked away.
>
> I can't expect you, or anyone else, to believe this at the present stage. But for myself I don't merely hope what I say, in my own mind I'm quite sure.

It may have been Keynes's lack of professional academic training[4] that led him to emphasise originality. Even allowing for the relatively primitive state of academic economics there was, certainly by the late 1920s and early 1930s and especially in the United States, a growing professional academic pattern of training emerging. For the academic economist this meant, *inter alia*, a doctorate in the subject,[5] a full-time academic post and continuous ongoing research typically with research staff support. Now Keynes was not like this at all. He had neither undergraduate nor graduate training in economics and his college appointment soon became almost secondary in his time commitment – most of his working week being spent in London as businessman and man of affairs in general.[6] Nor did Keynes engage in what we might term 'research' using the facilities of research assistants, quantitative techniques etc. As far as the latter is concerned, we know the hostility and suspicion with which Keynes approached the quantitative investigations that really got underway for the first time in the 1930s. His views came out most clearly in the correspondence surrounding his famous review of Tinbergen's *Testing Business Cycles.* Let me quote here at length from a letter he wrote to Sir Roy Harrod concerning the latter's presidential address to Section F of the British Association:[7]

> It seems to me that economics is a branch of logic, a way of thinking; and that you do not repel sufficiently firmly attempts *à la* Schultz to turn it into a pseudo-natural science. One can make some quite worthwhile progress merely by using your axioms and maxims. But one cannot get very far except by devising new and improved models. This requires, as you say, 'a vigilant observation of the actual working of our system'. Progress in economics consists almost entirely in a progressive improvement in the choice of models. The grave fault of the later classical school, exemplified by Pigou, has been to overwork a too simple or out-of-date model, and in not seeing that progress lay in improving the model; whilst Marshall often confused his models, for devising which he had great genius, by wanting to be realistic and by being unnecessarily ashamed of lean and abstract outlines.
>
> But it is of the essence of a model that one does not fill in real values for the variable functions. To do so would make it useless as a model. For as soon as this is done, the model loses its generality and its value as a mode of thought. That is why Clapham with his empty boxes was barking up the

wrong tree and why Schultz's results, if he ever gets any, are not very interesting (for we know beforehand that they will not be applicable to future cases). The object of statistical study is not so much to fill in missing variables with a view to prediction, as to test the relevance and validity of the model.

Economics is a science of thinking in terms of models joined to the art of choosing models which are relevant to the contemporary world. It is compelled to be this, because, unlike the typical natural science, the material to which it is applied is, in too many respects, not homogeneous through time. The object of a model is to segregate the semi-permanent or relatively constant factors from those which are transitory or fluctuating so as to develop a logical way of thinking about the latter, and of understanding the time sequences to which they give rise in particular cases.

Good economists are scarce because the gift for using 'vigilant observation' to choose good models, although it does not require a highly specialised intellectual technique, appears to be a very rare one.

In the second place, as against Robbins, economics is essentially a moral science and not a natural science. That is to say, it employs introspection and judgements of value.

Apart from his attack on the (then) rising star of econometrics,[8] another significant theme in the quoted passage is the emphasis on *theoretical* developments. In more recent language we may regard Keynes as thinking in terms of a paradigm change. It is this view of the development of economic reasoning that presents us with a clue to another aspect of Keynes's attitude to the classical tradition. This is an aspect which has not been mentioned much, if at all, in the literature – it is Keynes's absolute denunciation of the classical macro-tradition. His concern quite obviously was to destroy it and replace it with a new model. Rarely in the history of economics has the existing paradigm – and those who paraded it – been dealt with so harshly as Keynes did with the classics.

But who were these misguided classicists? At the opening of Chapter 1 of the *General Theory* we are told:[9]

'The classical economists' was a name invented by Marx to cover Ricardo and James Mill and their *predecessors*, that is to say for the founders of the theory which culminated in the Ricardian economics. I have become accustomed, perhaps perpetrating a solecism, to include in 'the classical school' the *followers* of Ricardo, those, that is to say, who adopted and perfected the theory of the Ricardian economics, including (for example) J. S. Mill, Marshall, Edgeworth and Professor Pigou.

What was the model of classical macroeconomics assumed by Keynes? This comes basically in the famous Chapter 2 of the *General Theory* – 'The Postulates of the Classical Economics'. He starts with the general proposition that classical economics assumes 'a given volume of employed resources',[10] although he does acknowledge exceptions. Indeed, as he points out, all discussions of economic fluctuations are concerned with an alternative assumption. Keynes also described this classical assumption as a belief in Say's Law which for him meant, 'in some significant, but not clearly defined, sense that the whole costs of production must necessarily be spent in the aggregate, directly or indirectly, in purchasing the product'.[11]

This basic assumption was, in its turn, based on 'two fundamental postulates', being:

(a) 'The wage is equal to the marginal product of labour.'
(b) 'The utility of the wage when a given volume of labour is employed is equal to the marginal disutility of that amount of employment.'[12]

In more recent terminology, postulate (a) means that hirers of labour time are on their demand curves, and postulate (b) that sellers of labour time are on their supply curves.[13]

This situation is compatible with frictional unemployment, defined by Keynes as 'unemployment due to a temporary want of balance between the relative quantities of specialised resources as a result of miscalculation or intermittent demand; or to time-lags consequent on unforeseen changes; or to the fact that the change-over from one employment to another cannot be effected without a certain delay, so that there will always exist in a non-static society a proportion of resources unemployed "between jobs" '.[14]

There is also voluntary unemployment which is 'due to the

refusal or inability of a unit of labour, as a result of legislation or social practices or of a response to change or mere human obstinacy, to accept a reward corresponding to the value of the product attributable to its marginal productivity'.[15]

Keynes chose to break out of 'classical' macroeconomics by rejecting the second postulate – 'we need to throw over the second postulate of the classical doctrine and to work out the behaviour of a system in which involuntary unemployment in the strict sense is possible'.[16]

So we now have the key notion of involuntary unemployment – a slippery concept to say the least. This is how Keynes himself defined it: 'Men are involuntarily unemployed if, in the event of a small rise in the price of wage–goods relatively to the money wage, both the aggregate supply of labour willing to work for the current money wage and the aggregate demand for it at that wage would be greater than the existing volume of employment'.[17]

The first postulate was still, however, accepted by Keynes and for him carried the same implications as in the classical model; namely that employment and the average real wage were negatively correlated.[18] What Keynes, of course, denied was that a reduction in money wages would lead *automatically* to a fall in real wages; in any case it was easier (he thought) to reduce real wages by increasing the money supply.

In spite of Keynes's continual use of the term 'classical' and his reference to writers such as Ricardo and J. S. Mill, the classical model presented and rejected in Keynes's *General Theory* is entirely that of the first three sections of Pigou's *Theory of Unemployment.*[19] This naturally raises a whole set of questions for the interpreter of this period. Why Pigou? Was Keynes fair to Pigou? Was Pigou representative of the existing state of macroeconomics and monetary economics?

Why Pigou? Well, of course, he was the 'Prof' and successor to Marshall.[20] For Keynes and his 'circus' it was the Cambridge tradition that had to be destroyed if the revolution was to succeed. And it was clearly Pigou that they were gunning for. The first clear evidence of conflict was when Pigou failed to see much that was new in the *Treatise.*[21] He writes to Keynes that he finds the analysis merely 'a variant that forms a more convenient skeleton than the Cambridge equation'.[22]

A few years later the *Theory of Unemployment* appears.

Immediately Keynes writes to Robertson (with a copy of the letter to Shove):[23]

> Have you read the Prof's book carefully? I find it most disturbing. For if I haven't completely misunderstood, it is simply nonsense from beginning to end.

Shove quickly replies to confirm Keynes's diagnosis:[24]

> It struck me as the worst book in economics that I had read for a long time – a good deal worse than Hicks.

**Was Keynes 'Fair' to Pigou?**

I have just referred to the fact that the main thrust of Keynes's attack – and to a considerable extent the 'circus' had the same end in view – was against the 'Prof', that is, Pigou. It is also clear that the break with D. H. Robertson was also due primarily to the fact that the latter would not abandon Pigou in the face of Keynes's hostility.[25]

We have argued that Keynes's model of classical economics comes entirely from Pigou's *Theory of Unemployment*. Is that work typical of Pigou's thought? We must presume that Keynes was relatively familiar with Pigou's other work and, of course, he had further means of assessing his work via the joint membership of certain crucial committees. In particular their membership of the Committee of Economists[26] (a subcommittee of the Economic Advisory Council) must have made them more than familiar with one another's views on unemployment and allied issues.

The publication of *The Theory of Unemployment* (1933) was not Pigou's first essay into unemployment problems to say the least. Indeed, as with his teacher Alfred Marshall, the dominant theme in his work was the problem of poverty and its amelioration; and a major cause of poverty was unemployment.

In *Wealth and Welfare* (1912) – later to become *The Economics of Welfare* (1920) – Pigou has sections discussing the evils of unemployment and the need to devise policies to ensure greater continuity of employment. Later editions of this book did not have these sections; instead, in his *Industrial Fluctuations* (1927) Pigou dealt separately with the trade cycle and unemployment. From his earliest writings Pigou maintained consistent support for a counter-cyclical public works policy. Moreover, even if we confine ourselves solely to the *Theory of Unemployment* (on the grounds that Keynes was simply concerned to demolish this particular work) we must note at least two things:

(1) Pigou emphasised that the book was not a complete treatment and that it had to be taken in conjunction with his other works. 'The work is thus tentative in character and, as no-one knows better than the author, in many respects unsatisfactory. Moreover, on a number of relevant matters, including some of the broader influence that govern movements of demand, I have said little. The reason is that they have already been discussed at length in my *Industrial Fluctuations*.'[27]

(2) Keynes summarises and criticises Pigou's 'real' analysis. But there is a Part IV and a Part V to Pigou's book. Part IV is entitled 'Monetary Factors Affecting Variations in the Level of the Real Demand Function for Labour'.[28] Part V is headed 'The Causation of Unemployment and of Changes in Unemployment'.[29]

I cannot here do justice to the full flavour of these two sections of the book but to give you some indication of what was missing from Keynes's account of it in the *General Theory* let me quote at some length from Part V Chapter 2. The subsection's title – which in itself should have given a clue to even the most impatient reader – is 'This, of course, is no argument against the temporary adoption of expansionist Government policies as "remedies" for unemployment in times of exceptional depressions'.[30] In this subsection Pigou writes:

> Our conclusion, that the long-run effect of expansionist State policies – and under this head must be included not only the undertakings of large-scale public works, but bounties, guarantees of interest, and, if successful in the purpose, protective duties – does not touch employment, affords, of course, no argument against the State's *temporarily* adopting these devices as 'remedies' for unemployment in times of exceptional depression. For here it is not their long-run, but their short-run, consequences that are significant. Nor need

we mean here by 'exceptional depression' merely the lower extremity of a normal trade cycle. Thus, though the heavy unemployment that prevailed in this country for the decade following the post-Armistice boom – the intractable million – was not associated with a cyclical depression in the narrow sense, there was, nevertheless, some reason to believe that it was a short-period malady, needing treatment for only a few difficult years. The situation was such that improvements in industrial technique and capital equipment might well have made the normal real demand for British labour expand at more than the usual rate, while, at the same time, owing to the low birth-rate of the pre-war, and, still more, of the war years, the number of the wage-earning population of working age was expanding at much less than the usual rate. This double change must clearly in the near future have made the absorption of the whole body of potential workers at a given wage-rate – real rate and money rate alike – much easier than it would otherwise have been. Thus a temporary campaign maintained for a few years – apart from the great slump that began in 1930 – might have proved successful.

Moreover, a lasting favourable effect on employment might be produced if the State undertook – and succeeded in its undertaking – not merely to make the real demand for labour higher than it would otherwise have been, but to make it progressively higher.

I hope that enough has been said to convince you that Keynes's treatment of Pigou in the *General Theory* was grossly unfair. Why did Keynes adopt this strategy – as he did incidentally against other members of the Cambridge school? The reasons are complex; part of the explanation lies in personality clashes. The main point to note – as we have before – is that Keynes wanted a *theoretical* victory by which I mean that he wanted a confession from his apparent opponents that their theory had been wrong and that he (Keynes) had 'discovered' a more appropriate theoretical model of capitalism.

Although Keynes professed to be overwhelmingly interested in policy change and in his dealings with politicians this was indeed the case, nonetheless in academic circles his goal was theoretical revolution and claims to originality and 'newness'. Pigou was just wrong and he had to 'confess' – which indeed he did in a set of lectures in 1949.[31]

**The Classical Economists**

Now I turn to what we had better call the 'classical economists' proper. By time-period I have in mind the 100 years from 1750–1850, and by name the key figures of Hume, Smith, Ricardo, Senior and J. S. Mill. Those who are experts on the classical economics will already, at this stage, wish to tear this list apart and for many purposes this would indeed be the appropriate way to proceed. However, for our purposes – as I shall indicate – the list is best kept together. It is true, of course, that if we are investigating the classical school's attitude towards the determinants and limitations of the growth process we would have to distinguish fairly strongly between the broad optimism of Smith, with its patent overtures of increasing returns to scale and the apparition of the stationary state well to the background, and the views of Ricardo and J. S. Mill. The latter two, Ricardo particularly, wrote at times as if the stationary state were just round the corner. They were also less sure of the engine of growth and indeed Ricardo never convinced himself that economists could say much about the size of national income, only its factor distribution in the development process – an observation incidentally which drew praise from Keynes who otherwise viewed Ricardo as fundamentally misguided.

It is true as well that if we were investigating value and distribution theory in the classical period we would need to make some fairly sharp distinctions between the writers mentioned above. Indeed, to put the matter more generally it is a matter of some considerable doubt as to where we place the alleged unity of classical thought. In value theory? Growth theory? Economic policy? None of these candidates really stand up to the test of sustained scholarship and research.

However, I do think we find a unity if we focus on their macroeconomic analysis, by which I mean specifically and explicitly their theory of the demand for labour and the determination of the volume of employment.

To put the classical analysis on its most basic, fundamental terms it is most appropriately described as an 'advances' theory of capital. Whilst there are indeed exceptions and modifications to this simple model, nonetheless unless we keep this vision to the forefront we miss the central theme. Moreover, this theme is common from Smith to the late classical period so that we have some 100 years of common doctrine. This is why I have always preferred to see the unity of classical doctrine in its macro-analysis rather than in value and distribution theory or in some alleged fixation with the dogma of *laissez-faire*.

The structure of this advances model (or 'corn' model – as some may wish to describe it) may be stated below:

*Assumptions*

(a) output is assumed to consist (entirely) of wage goods, that is, commodities that enter into the typical worker's household budget;
(b) the production function for wage goods is of the fixed point input–output type and roughly coincides with the agricultural period of production;
(c) the workers are assumed *not* to save hence their consumption depends solely on wages. In order to survive during the production period they have to be 'advanced' wages ahead of output;
(d) employers of labour ('capitalists', 'farmers') are the only savers in the system. They receive the whole output at the end of each production period ('harvest') and allocate it between personal household consumption and saving;
(e) capital is basically variable capital.

*Analytics*

Let us start at the beginning of a product period. Output, that is, the stock of wage goods, will be in the hands of capitalist farmers. Some they will have (notionally) allocated for their own consumption, the rest will be a 'wages fund' for the employment and support of labour during the current period of production. What does this tell us about the demand for labour? Well, very simply if the *ex ante* division between capitalist consumption and capitalist saving is the *ex post* one, the demand for labour reduces to the 'wages fund' divided by the given real wage. Alternatively, if the real wage is a variable – which would be the case if there were no individual labour supply functions, just the desire to work for any positive wage – the volume of employment would be given by the fixed supply, and the size of the wages fund will determine the average real wage.

*Implications of the Model*

Actually, there are many. Some are not our direct concern so I will now list those which are particularly for our attention.

(a) Saving and investment are the same activity. There is no need for any mechanism to equate the decisions to save and invest, be it the rate of interest in classical models or the level of income in Keynesian models.
(b) It therefore follows that the crucial decision variable is the capitalists' propensity to save. It is this that, given the volume of output and the real wage, determines the volume of employment.
(c) Any increase in current consumption must lead, *in the current production period*, to either a fall in the real wage or a decrease in employment.
(d) Government expenditure cannot increase the current demand for labour.
(e) The demand for labour is downward sloping with respect to the real wage.

There is, of course, a considerable stock of amplifications and modifications that the central classical writers added themselves to this *simpliste* model. We shall outline the major ones shortly. First though, to illustrate the key place of the model, we shall look at our analysis with reference to two dominant sources taken from the beginning and end of the classical period. We choose Book II of the *Wealth of Nations* and J. S. Mill's famous Chapter V 'Fundamental Propositions Respecting Capital' from the *Principles*.

Smith starts with the central proposition that the output of wage goods is solely a function of the number of productive labourers:[32]

> Both productive and unproductive labourers, and those who do not labour at all, are all equally maintained by the annual produce of the land and labour of the country. . . Accordingly. . . as a smaller or greater proportion of it is in any one year employed in maintaining unproductive hands, the more in the one case and the less in the other will remain for the

productive, and the next year's produce will be the greater or smaller accordingly.

How is the capital stock (annual wages fund) to be increased?

Parsimony, and not industry is the immediate cause of the increase of capital. . . if parsimony did not save and store up, the capital would never be the greater.[33]

And, of course, this saving is automatically invested hence there is no leakage from the circular flow of income.

What is annually saved is as regularly consumed as what is annually spent, and nearly at the same time too; but it is consumed by a different set of people.[34]

From this it followed that government expenditure could never increase the wages fund and hence the demand for labour because it was unproductive expenditure. Thus from the point of view of macro-policy there was no need to interfere with market forces.

The uniform, constant, and uninterrupted effort of every man to better his condition, the principle from which public and national, as well as private opulence is originally derived, is frequently powerful enough to maintain the natural progress of things towards improvement, in spite of both of the extravagance of government, and of the greatest errors of administration. Like the unknown principle of animal life, it frequently restores health and vigour to the constitution, in spite, not only of the disease but of the absurd prescriptions of the doctor.[35]

John Stuart Mill's statement of the basic model is seen with the utmost clarity if we simply list his 'propositions'.

(1) 'Industry is limited by capital'.
(2) 'Capital is the result of saving'.
(3) 'All capital is consumed'.
(4) 'Demand for commodities is not a demand for labour'.

It is the fourth proposition that always causes the shock, and one's initial reaction is to assume that the 'not' must be deleted. However, if we remember our advances model then all the propositions follow. And the interpretation of the fourth proposition is simply that, within the advances model, an increase in current consumption demand cannot increase the wages fund hence cannot increase the demand for labour.

**Modifications of the Central Classical Position**

Even within the orthodox camp there was a host of literature modifying and amending the basic model. How far a conscious, full acceptance of these amendments, and their significance for the central tenets of classical thought, should have led the faithful to abandon their position on such issues as the demand for labour, causes of unemployment, neutrality of money etc., is a very difficult question to answer even with hindsight. As I have argued elsewhere[36] it is doubtful whether an alternative paradigm in the field of short-run macroeconomics was available to the classical writers. Whether this was so or not, the plain facts of the matter are that when the cards were down the classical writers would have no truck whatsoever with the unorthodox even though in other circumstances they more than flirted with them. By the 'cards were down', I mean situations of practical policy discussion where the unorthodox looked for support for their ideas to the accepted establishment orthodoxy.

For the classical economists 'proper' the main areas where modifications were clearly stated were as follows:

(1) the non-neutrality of money supply changes in the short run;
(2) the transmission mechanism of money supply to economic activity via interest rate changes;
(3) the distinction between a saving class and an investor class;
(4) the difference between a barter and a monetary economy.

It goes without saying that this is an important list and we shall now present the major elements under each heading. Note that items (1) and (2) bear most directly on the Keynesian position because they refer to propositions that are usually alleged to be central to the theoretical structure of the *General Theory* and quite the negation of classical thinking. Keynesian economics – by which I do *not* mean the neoclassical synthesis – is supposed to show (a) the non-neutrality of money, (b) that the only link between money and economic activity is via interest rates, and (c) that a central feature of capitalism is the distinction between the decision to save and the decision to invest.

*Non-neutrality of money*

By this we shall mean that, at least in the short run, changes in the quantity of money affect (some of the) real variables in the system. Apart from the reasoning which we deal with under (2) there are two main reasons why certain classical writers accepted the fact that changes in the supply of money would affect economic activity and not just engender a parallel change in all prices. First there was the assumption that idle resources existed. Now here we must tread cautiously before we jump to the conclusion that certain key figures (for example David Hume whom we shall quote below) accepted the 'fact' of involuntary unemployment. In the later 'Mercantilist' literature of the late seventeenth and early eighteenth century it was fairly commonplace to assume that an increase in total spending would call forth an increase in output via an increase in employment. References to such sources as William Petty's *Treatise on Taxes and Contributions* and Bishop Berkeley's *The Querist* are well documented in the literature.

Hume, in his *Political Discourses* (1752), certainly makes it very clear that the initial effect of an increase in the quantity of money – which he assumes leads directly to an increase in effective demand for output – is on output and hours worked rather than on prices. Moreover, the straightforward neutrality of the 'pure' quantity theory is seen as a long-run 'comparative static' proposition. The best example of his reasoning here is to be found in the essay 'Of Money'.

Hume's economic analysis is particularly interesting because there we find both an attempt to work out the comparative statics of full equilibrium states – a methodology often associated *par excellence* with neoclassical writers – and a brave attempt to work out the process of disequilibrium behaviour between positions of successive equilibria. It may be said, with more than a grain of justice, and certainly with little offence to historical scholarship, that the understanding of short-run macro-behaviour would have developed a good deal faster if readers of Hume had concentrated more on his disequilibrium economics rather than on his propositions in comparative statics. The latter propositions are unambiguously stated both in 'Of Money' and 'Of the Balance of Trade', for example:

> If we consider any one kingdom by itself, it is evident, that the greater or less plenty of money is of no consequence; since the prices of commodities are always proportioned to the plenty of money.[37]

Or again,

> Suppose four-fifths of all the money in Great Britain to be annihilated in one night, and the nation reduced to the same condition, with regard to specie, as in the reigns of the Harrys and Edwards, what would be the consequence? Must not the price of all labour and commodities sink in proportion, and everything be sold as cheap as they were in those ages? . . . Again, suppose, that all the money of Great Britain were multiplied fivefold in a night, must not the contrary effect follow.[38]

But all of that refers to a position of full adjustment after the disturbance. In disequilibrium we find Hume arguing:

> In my opinion, it is only in this interval or intermediate situation, between the acquisition of money and rise of prices, that the increasing quantity of gold and silver is favourable to industry. . . Here are a set of manufacturers or merchants, we shall suppose, who have received returns of gold and silver for goods which they sent to Cadiz. They are thereby enabled to employ more workmen than formerly, who never dream of demanding higher wages, but are glad of employment from such good paymasters. If workmen become scarce, the manufacturer gives higher wages, but at first requires an increase of labour; and this is willingly submitted to by the artisan who can now eat and drink

better, to compensate his additional toil and fatigue. He carries his money to market, where he finds everything at the same price as formerly, but returns with greater quantity and of better kinds, for the use of his family. The farmer and gardener, finding that all their commodities are taken off, apply themselves with alacrity to the raising of more; and at the same time can afford to take better and more cloths from their tradesmen, whose price is the same as formerly, and their industry only whetted by so much new gain. It is easy to trace the money in its progress through the whole commonwealth; where we shall find that it must first quicken the diligence of every individual, before it increased the price of labour.[39]

The second feature of non-neutrality concerns the rather more complex doctrine of 'forced saving'. In its pure form this concept does not involve the assumption of idle resources either in its open or disguised form. It assumes rather that incomes – and more specifically money wages – adjust less rapidly than prices to changes in spending induced by changes in the quantity of money. Thus with an increase in the general level of prices, working-class consumption is cut and hence real investment may increase. This doctrine, which appears to have been first stated by Saint Peravy (1786), is also clearly enunciated by such straightforward classical writers as Thornton, Torrens and Ricardo. Henry Thornton, for example, in *Paper Credit* develops it as follows, having initially made it clear that he also recognises the 'Hume' effect:

> It (i.e. an increase in the quantity of money) may be imagined either, first, to be used in transferring an increased quantity of articles, which it must, in that case, be assumed that the new paper itself has tended to create; or, secondly, in transferring the same articles at a higher price.[40]

The first possibility is the one we have already alluded to, using Hume as our source, as indeed does Thornton.[41] On the second possibility he argues as follows:

> It must be admitted, that, provided we assume an excessive issue of paper to lift up, as it may for a time, the cost of

goods, though not the price of labour, some augmentation of stock will be the consequence; for the labourer, according to this supposition, may be forced by his necessity to consume fewer articles, though he may exercise the same industry. But this saving, as well as any additional one which may arise from a similar defalcation of the revenue of the unproductive members of the society, will be attended with a proportionate hardship and injustice.

*The transmission mechanism*

There can be no doubt that a central proposition of classical thought was that in full equilibrium changes in the quantity of money had no effect on the rate of interest. This is stated categorically throughout the classical period; we find it in Hume, Smith, Ricardo and J. S. Mill, for example. However, this did not answer the question how money affected prices and economic activity generally. There are hints of a 'direct' or 'real balance effect' mechanism[42] but the main emphasis is placed on short-run changes in the rate of interest and hence on the demand for investible funds. Thornton again is absolutely clear on this point but we can be even more orthodox than this and quote Ricardo from his evidence before a Lords Committee.[43]

> Reduction or Increase of the Quantity of Money always ultimately raises or lowers the Price of Commodities; when this is effected, the Rate of Interest will be precisely the same as before; it is only during the Interval, that is, before the Prices are settled at their new Rate, that the Rate of Interest is either raised or lowered.

This analysis is then linked in classical thought to the relationship between the rate of interest and the demand for investible funds, hence the total transmission mechanism is established.

*The distinction between the decision to save and the decision to invest*

It is commonly said that a central landmark on the way to Keynesville is the recognition of a distinction between the decision to save – typically by households – and the decision to invest – typically by an entrepreneurial group. Of itself, recognition of the two separate decisions is not sufficient to lead us into Keynesian problems – we have to add a theory as to why the process of plan coordination is not achieved *ex ante* by some regulatory device – however it is obviously a fair leap forward from the rather primitive 'saving is investment' assumption of the 'advances' model. As an example of a staunch Ricardian dealing with this question we choose William Ellis in an article which appeared anonymously in the *Westminster Review* (1825).[44] First the motives to save, these exist:

> totally independent of any addition which might be made to the savings themselves. The inducement to save a sum of money for fourteen years is no doubt considerably strengthened by the knowledge that the sum saved will be doubled at the end of that period; but even where no profit is superadded, where the sum of money at the expiration of the fourteen years is no greater than the sum originally laid by, savings would still be made. . .[45]

and he concludes:

> *The motives to save, independent of any pecuniary profit. . . are stronger in a civilised than in a barbarous age.*[46] (A very Keynesian statement!)

Next come the motives to invest:

> The higher the rate of profit in any community, the greater will be the portion of the annual savings which is added to capital; and the greater will be the inducement to save. The lower the rate of profit, the smaller will be the portion of the annual savings which is added to capital.

The rate of interest is assumed to act as the *ex ante* equilibriator but even so the analysis is a long way on from the basic model.

*The demand for money and the differences between a barter and a monetary economy*

Part of the 'New Keynesian' message is to reassert the crucial distinction between a barter economy with some sort of token money grafted on, and a fully fledged monetary economy where (Knightian) uncertainty prevails. Along with this movement has been a growing recognition of the sterility of general equilibrium theory as an approach to sensible macroeconomics. Whilst it is quite legitimate to argue that the classical writers saw no essential differences between a barter and a monetary economy and hence regarded money 'as a veil' masking, to the uninitiated, the essential exchange of commodities for commodities, nonetheless we do get a statement to the contrary in the classical literature. The prime example of this most Keynesian-like approach to be found in the orthodox classical literature comes, as is now well known, in the famous essay of J. S. Mill entitled 'Of the Influence of Consumption on Production'.[47]

The *Essay* – somewhat ironically – is an attempt to refute notions of the possibility of general overproduction. But having laid out at great length the truism of Say's Law in a barter economy, Mill suddenly changes track in the last three pages.

> The argument is evidently founded on the supposition of a state of barter. . . If, however, we suppose that money is used, these propositions cease to be exactly true. It must be admitted that no person desires money for its own sake and that he who sells his commodity, receiving money in exchange, does so with the intention of buying with that same money some other commodity. Interchange by means of money is therefore, as has often been observed, ultimately nothing but barter. But there is this difference – that in the case of barter, the selling and buying are simultaneously conpounded in one operation; you sell what you have, and buy what you want, by one indivisible act, and you cannot do the one without doing the other. Now the effect of the employment of money, and even the utility of it, is that it enables this one act of interchange to be divided into two separate acts or operations; one of which may be performed now, and the other a year hence, or whenever it shall be most convenient. Although he who sells, really sells only to buy, he need not buy at the same moment when he sells, and does not therefore necessarily add to the *immediate* demand for one commodity – when he adds to the supply of the other. The buying and selling being now separated, it may very well

occur, that there may be, at some given time, a very general inclination to sell with as little delay as possible, accompanied with an equally general inclination to defer all purchases as long as possible. This is always actually the case, in those periods which are described as periods of general excess. . . what (is) called a general superabundance was not a superabundance of all commodities relatively to commodities, but a superabundance of all commodities relatively to money. What it amounted to was, that persons in general, at that particular time, from a general expectation of being called upon to meet sudden demands, liked better to possess money than any other commodity.[48]

One may well ask whether, if the *Essay* had been more widely read and understood, a good deal of subsequent debate and controversy would have been necessary.

What I have tried to argue so far is that whether we take Keynes's interpretation of classical macroeconomics as being Pigovian or 'real' classical, the account that he gave of their doctrines was inadequate. Why he chose to do this we have briefly mentioned and will return to later. Now, however, we need to ask whether Keynes had classical connections in a more general sense.

**Did Keynes Reject the Liberal Tradition?**

To the extent to which Keynes overthrew classical macroeconomics, (although, as we have seen the phrase neoclassical macroeconomics is perhaps more appropriate) he clearly rejected a central piece of classical, liberal thought. But how central was it? Did it imply, *ipso facto*, a rejection of classical thought? I think not. It seems absurd to believe that, for example, Adam Smith, John Stuart Mill or Alfred Marshall would have found the advocacy of full employment policies along 'Keynesian' lines incompatible with their liberal faith. To answer our question sensibly we must enumerate what we take to be the economic basis of classical liberalism and see how far Keynes, even under the impact of his changing macroeconomic vision, still remained of that persuasion. The economic bases of classical liberalism may be put in terms of the following set of propositions:

(1) That, with certain exceptions, the market is an efficient allocative mechanism.
(2) That private property is an essential ingredient of the market system.
(3) That profits are an essential reward for the operation of the market system.
(4) That there is nothing particularly optimal about the *status quo* distribution of income and wealth in any society and these distributions might usefully be moved towards greater equality, provided no hindrance to economic efficiency is experienced.
(5) That economic dealings should be as free from restrictions as possible, in other words free trade was to be the *normal* rule of (international) trade.

Now Keynes's views on such matters are usually culled from his *The End of Laissez-Faire*[49] and the final chapter in the *General Theory*,[50] although we also have his essay on *Am I a Liberal?*[51] We use here the *General Theory* as a testament of Keynes's last 'official' statement of his views although there are other hints as to his philosophy towards the last few years of his life.[52]

(1) To put the point correctly, I see no reason to suppose that the existing system seriously misemploys the factors of production which are in use. There are, of course, errors of foresight; but these would not be avoided by central decisions. When 9 000 000 men are employed out of 10 000 000 willing and able to work, there is no evidence that the labour of these 9 000 000 is misdirected. The complaint against the present system is not that these 9 000 000 men ought to be employed on different tasks, but that tasks should be available for the remaining 1 000 000 men. It is in determining the volume, not the direction, of actual employment that the existing system has broken down.[53]

(2) There are valuable human activities which require the motive of money-making and the environment of private wealth-ownership for their full fruition.[54]
Individualism, if it can be purged of its defects and

its abuses is the best safeguard of personal liberty.[55]

(3) Thus we might aim in practice at an increase in the volume of capital until it ceases to be scarce, so that the functionless investor will no longer receive a bonus; and at a scheme of direct taxation which allows the intelligence and determination and executive skill of the financier, the entrepreneur *et hoc genus omne* to be harnessed to the service of the community on reasonable terms of reward.[56]

(4) there are certain justifications for inequality of incomes which do not apply equally to inequality of inheritances. For my own part, I believe that there is social and psychological justification for significant inequalities of income and wealth, but not for such large disparities as exist today.[57]

(5) if nations can learn to provide themselves with full employment by their domestic policy there need be no important economic forces calculated to set the interest of one country against that of its neighbours. There would still be room for the international division of labour and for international lending in appropriate conditions. . . International trade would cease to be what it is, namely, a desperate expedient to maintain employment at home by forcing sales on foreign markets and restricting purchases, which, if successful, will merely shift the problem of unemployment to the neighbour which is worsened in the struggle, but a willing and unimpeded exchange of goods and services in conditions of mutual advantage.[58]

So basically Keynes wanted to wed full employment to classical liberalism both as a politicoeconomic policy and as a method of analysis.

If we suppose the volume of output to be given, i.e. to be determined by forces outside the classical scheme of thought, then there is no objection to be raised against the classical analysis of the manner in which private self-interest will determine what in particular is produced, in what proportions the factors of production will be combined to produce it, and how the value of the final output will be distributed between them.[59]

This interpretation of Keynes as essentially an economic liberal arguing for specific non-liberal measures solely in periods of unemployment is borne out, it seems to me, by the attitude of certain members of the Labour party in the early 1940s towards Keynes's negotiations with the United States. Michael Foot, for example, in his biography of Nye Bevan writes:

> He (Bevan) would not acknowledge Keynes as the great economic prophet of the new age. He had never been prepared to accept Keynes's analysis as a substitute for a fuller Socialist criterion of capitalist society, and he had never been convinced that Keynesian techniques would be adequate to cure the disease. Now Keynes, for all his toughness and skill in negotiations, had revealed how much he was attracted by a considerable part of the American case; he was reverting in part to his earliest liberalism. . . Bevan feared that if ever the world was launched on the free trade flood, which both the Americans and Keynes envisaged, Socialist Britain would be swamped in the process.[60]

**A Keynesian Revolution Without Keynes?**

I have argued so far that Keynes was politically and philosophically within the classical tradition and that whilst he vehemently rejected classical and neoclassical macroeconomics his version of it was tantamount to a 'straw man'. Indeed, that simple picture of 'life before Keynes' that I drew for you at the beginning of this seminar owes much to Keynes himself!

But what of the unorthodox or 'Keynesian' literature prior to Keynes? Could all of this have added up to a Keynesian revolution? Apart from the underworld economics of economists such as Malthus, J. M. Robertson, Hobson, Gesell, Douglas and the like, there are two other traditions that must be serious contenders. First there is the Marxist tradition stemming from Marx's own analysis of *Departments* and developed by a long line of followers from Rosa Luxemburg to Michael Kalecki.[61]

Secondly we have the Swedish School launched by Wicksell

and continued through Myrdal, Lindahl, Ohlin, Lundberg and Palander. How far these members of the 'Stockholm School' were independent discoverers of the Keynesian message is still a matter of some dispute. What cannot be denied, however, is that the fate they overwhelmingly met in the UK and the USA was one of complete neglect.[62] By the time translations of their major works were made available in English, Keynes's *General Theory* had swamped all other contributions and in any case the initial Keynesian reaction to the Swedish School was rather hostile.[63]

As a third stream of thought that might well have led on to quite radical modifications of the basic classical and neoclassical position, we must mention the Cambridge School itself. I do not mean here the obvious and now well-documented importance of the 'circus' in contributing to the vital changes in Keynes's thinking from the *Treatise on Money* (1930) to the *General Theory*. Rather, I refer to the more direct Cambridge tradition of Marshall himself coming to fruition in Pigou, Hawtrey, Lavington and (especially) D. H. Robertson.[64]

Now it is beyond my purpose here to trace out these possibilities of a Keynesian revolution without Keynes. But as a prelude to such a study we must have some sort of agreement about the nature of the revolution itself; the question we then seek to pose is not 'was there a Keynesian revolution' but rather 'what was the Keynesian revolution'! This dramatic change in the nature of the question to be asked may appear paradoxical to us but is nothing but a reflection of the fact that, in my view, controversy about the nature of the Keynesian revolution and the true worth of Keynes's analysis and diagnosis in the *General Theory*, is greater today than at any time since its publication in 1936. We currently have two extreme and basically irreconcilable views on Keynes's contribution. Dominating, although (as it appears to me) losing ground daily, is what is known as the neoclassical synthesis or – to use a more figurative expression – 'bastard Keynesianism'. This interpretation rejects Keynes's central claim of a general theory and rather subsumes his model as a special case applicable, if at all, to extreme slump conditions and depending for its significance on institutional factors like wage rigidity rather than on any path-breaking theoretical innovation. Key names along this interpretive path are Hicks, Modigliani and Patinkin.[65]

At the other extreme in our interpretation of Keynes, we have the 'fundamentalists' who continue to assert the irreconcilability of Keynes's views with the neoclassical tradition. Keynes, in this scenario, destroyed the legitimacy of Say's Law in a capitalist economy and demonstrated the basic irrationality of such a system. Keynes and neoclassical thought cannot be brought together on the menu of the café ISL(A)M via gentle combinations of fiscal and monetary policies. The lineage for this rendering includes G. L. S. Shackle, Joan Robinson, R. F. Harrod, N. Kaldor, A. Leijonhufvud, R. Clower and P. Davidson.[66]

Where did Keynes stand in all of this? Was he a Keynesian or a neoclassical synthesiser? Actually this is a very difficult question to answer. Selected quotations from the *General Theory* give credence to both extremes of interpretation: Keynes himself added to the confusion by giving support to practically anyone who reviewed his book sympathetically – certainly he underwrote, for example, Hicks' mathematical account of the *General Theory*[67] which is often regarded as forming the core of the Keynesian counterrevolution.

It is possible, of course, that Keynes himself did not fully understand the import of this own ideas – a not uncommon occurrence in highly creative work.[68] Whilst I think it is possible to reject categorically the simple 45-degree cross-approach as being Keynes's view – especially that central textbook assumption of a *fixed-price* world until full employment is reached – it is harder to support the view that Keynes was a 'Keynesian' in the current radical sense. As we have seen in the previous section of this paper his model was very much 'capitalism plus full employment' and he was relatively sanguine about the feasibility of macro-control.

But whatever our view of the Keynesian revolution and how far Keynes himself understood it, there is no question that he wanted to spawn a revolution. He wanted a dramatic change in economic thinking – and he wanted it fast. This leads us to the last question on our agenda.

### What is the Best Way to Change Economic Ideas?

It is tempting to ask whether the reception accorded to Keynesian economics and especially its influence on policy – which some commentators feel was the only possible line towards improvement in the early and mid-1930s – would have been eased if Keynes, and his immediate followers, had adopted somewhat different tactics in debate.

Keynes's concern was to change economic thought because, rightly or wrongly, he believed that this was the way to engender a permanent change in policy.[69] So what is the best way to engender idea shifts in economics?

Looking at the history of economics it seems to me that we observe two broad ways in which efforts have been made to change the corpus of economic reasoning. We may label these: (*a*) the continuity view; and (*b*) the discontinuity view.[70]

In (*a*) I include writers who emphasise the continuity of thought and play down the revolutionary element in their own contributions. In this group are to be included, as I have already suggested, Ricardo, J. S. Mill, Marshall and D. H. Robertson (and in our own day H. G. Johnson). Group (*b*) writers require of us complete breaks with the past – Smith, Jevons and Keynes are obvious candidates here – and of this company it is Keynes who stands out as the iconoclast *par excellence*. We have seen how it permeated the *General Theory* and this also accounts for the fact that Keynes dealt very severely with any economist, however sympathetic to his (Keynes's) views, who attempted any *rapprochement* with the classical or neoclassical writers. Let me quote again from the Harrod–Keynes correspondence where Keynes is writing to Harrod about the latter's proposed review of the *General Theory*:

> I am frightfully afraid of the tendency, of which I see some signs in you, to appear to accept my constructive part and to find some accommodation between this and deeply cherished views which would, in fact, only be possible if my constructive part has been partially misunderstood. That is to say, I expect a good deal of what I write to be water off a duck's back. I am certain that it will be water off a duck's back unless I am sufficiently strong in my criticism to force the classics to make rejoinders. I want, so to speak, to raise a dust; because it is only out of the controversy that will arise that what I am saying will get understood.[71]

H. G. Johnson, in his discussion of revolutionary tactics in economics, suggests at least two conditions to be a successful revolutionary:

(1) the new ideas must be too difficult for the old guard to comprehend easily and readily;
(2) the ideas must be sufficiently easy for the young Turks to grasp.[72]

Now there are two main ways of ensuring that condition (1) is fulfilled; first by using mathematical techniques unknown to the old guard; second by using new terminology, or old terminology in new ways, and maximising the (apparent) difference between the new and the old ideas. This strategy prevents the old guard assimilating the new ideas onto their own reference patterns. Hence when they do convert it has to be total.

Keynes seems to have been a successful revolutionary although, as I have been at pains to emphasise, our evaluation here will depend on our assessment of the *essential message* of Keynes's economics. Keynes, in a very real sense, wrote his own place in the history of economics – he invented the popular or textbook account of the development of macroeconomics. As I have tried to indicate, his narrative will not stand the weight of historical scholarship. However, he did it with a purpose and that was to speed the change of ideas – the paradigm switch in Kuhnian phraseology. His whole personality, upbringing, social and intellectual environment also reinforced newness and originality.

Whether this invented history of economics and Keynes's revolutionary tactics were, as they say, in the public interest remains a moot point.

NOTES

1. For those readers who would like a really good statement of the 'Treasury View' here is one:

> the additional £125m a year required for new state or local authority borrowing cannot be found without impinging on the supply of capital for other home requirements. . . The large loans, if they are not to involve inflation, must draw on existing capital resources. These resources are, on the whole, utilised at present in varying degrees of active employment; and the great bulk is utilised for home

investment/commercial purposes. The extent to which any additional employment could be given by altering the direction of investment is, therefore, at the best strictly limited. But the direction of investment can only be altered if we are prepared to offer sufficiently high money rates to counteract the attractions offered. If, however, we do so, the damage done to home trade and employment by the imposition of such high rates would undoubtedly be much greater than any benefit they could obtain from the funds that could thereby be diverted from foreign investment.
Cmd. 3331 (May 1929).

2. Cmd. 6527 (1944).

3. From a letter to George Bernard Shaw, 1 January 1935 in *Collected Writings of John Maynard Keynes*, Vol. XIII, pp. 492–3.

This 'originality syndrome' is apparent in Keynes from his earliest work on business fluctuations. His first contribution to this area was a paper presented to the Political Economy Club in 1913 entitled 'How Far are Bankers Responsible for the Alternatives of Crisis and Depression?'. Writing of this paper to D. H. Robertson – whose *A Study of Industrial Fluctuations* he had just read – Keynes states, 'Your work has suggested to me what appears at first sight a superb theory about fluctuations', and in the paper itself we read 'the object of this paper is to see what the club thinks of a general explanation of fluctuations which is to some extent novel'. *Collected Writings*, Vol. XIII, pp. 1–2.

4. Plus, of course, membership of the Bloomsbury Group where, it often appears, originality was the sole criterion of importance.

5. For example, Chamberlin, Knight, Taussig, Viner.

6. cf. D. E. Moggridge, *Keynes* (1976), Chapter 4.

7. *Collected Writings*, Vol. XIV, pp. 296–7.

8. The Econometric Society was founded in 1930 mainly through the efforts of Irving Fisher and Ragnor Frisch.

9. *The General Theory of Employment, Interest and Money* (1936), p. 3 footnote.

10. Ibid., p. 4.

11. Ibid., p. 18. Here Keynes quotes J. S. Mill and Marshall in support of this interpretation.

12. Ibid., p. 5.

13. Thus all action is 'voluntary'.

14. *General Theory*, p. 6.

15. Ibid., p. 6.

16. Ibid., p. 16. We now have involuntary action in the model. This creates problems for the use of the concept of equilibrium and it led to what must now be regarded as a fruitless debate about whether involuntary unemployment was compatible with equilibrium. It all depends on how one uses the term 'equilibrium'.

17. Ibid., p. 15.

18. 'In a given state of organisation, equipment and technique, the real wage earned by a unit of labour has a unique (inverse) correlation with the volume of employment' (*General Theory*, p. 17). The fact that real wages

seem to move procyclically was one of the earliest 'empirical' criticisms of the *General Theory*. We can either abandon the assumption of diminishing marginal productivity or develop the Keynesian assumptions in a formal model of disequilibrium behaviour. For the latter approach see, for example, D. Patinkin, *Money, Interest and Prices* (2nd edition, 1965) Chapters 13 and 14; R. Barro and H. Grossman, *Money, Employment and Inflation* (1976).

19. A. C. Pigou, *The Theory of Unemployment* (1933).

20. Pigou succeeded Marshall as Professor of Political Economy in 1908. In turn he was succeeded by D. H. Robertson in 1941.

21. J. M. Keynes, *A Treatise on Money* (1930) and *Collected Writings.*

22. Letter to J. M. Keynes (May 1931); *Collected Writings*, Vol. XIII, p. 217.

23. Letter to D. H. Robertson, 5 September 1933, Ibid., Vol. XIII, p. 310.

24. Letter to J. M. Keynes, 23 September 1933, Ibid., Vol. XIII, p. 321.

25. Robertson's loyalty comes out very clearly in the Keynes–Robertson correspondence about Pigou's *Theory of Unemployment.* See also the article 'Arthur Cecil Pigou' by E. A. G. Robinson in the *International Encyclopaedia of the Social Sciences*, Vol. XII (1968).

26. On this point see S. Howson and D. Winch, *The Economic Advisory Council 1930–1939* (1977).

27. A. C. Pigou, op. cit., pp. vi–vii.

28. Ibid., pp. 185–246.

29. Ibid., pp. 247–314.

30. Ibid., p. 247.

31. They were published as *Keynes' General Theory: A Retrospective View* (1950).

32. A. Smith, *The Wealth of Nations* (Cannan edition) Vol. II, p. 314.

33. Ibid., Vol. II, p. 320.

34. Ibid., Vol. II, p. 320.

35. Ibid., Vol. II, p. 325.

36. B. A. Corry, *Money, Saving and Investment* (London, 1962).

37. David Hume, *Writings on Economics* (ed. E. Rotwein, London, 1955), p. 33.

38. Ibid., pp. 62–3.

39. Ibid., p. 38.

40. H. Thornton, *An Enquiry into the Nature and Effects of the Paper Credit of Great Britain* (ed. F. A. Hayek, New York, 1939), p. 235.

41. Ibid., p. 238.

42. See D. Patinkin, *Money, Interest, and Prices*, p. 529.

43. D. Ricardo, *Collected Works*, Vol. V (Cambridge, 1953).

44. 'The Effects of the Employment of Machinery. . . Upon the Happiness of the Working Class', *Westminster Review*, Vol. V, p. 105 *et seq.*

45. Ibid., p. 106.

46. Ibid., p. 107.

47. *Collected Works of John Stuart Mill* (Toronto edition), Vol. IV, p.

263 *et seq.*

48. Ibid., p. 276 or 277.

49. *The End of Laissez-Faire* (1926) first given as the Sidney Bell Lecture at Oxford in 1924; *Collected Writings*, Vol. IX, p. 272 *et seq.*

50. The final chapter of the *General Theory* is entitled 'Concluding Notes on the Social Philosophy towards which the General Theory Might Lead'.

51. First published in the *Nation and Athenaeum* (1925); *Collected Writings*, Vol. IX, p. 295 *et seq.*

52. See R. F. Harrod, *Life of John Maynard Keynes* (London, 1951).

53. *General Theory*, p. 379.

54. Ibid., p. 374.

55. Ibid., p. 380.

56. Ibid., pp. 376–7.

57. Ibid., pp. 373–4.

58. Ibid., pp. 382–3.

59. Ibid., pp. 378–9.

60. Michael Foot, *Aneurin Bevan 1945–60* (London, 1973), p. 56.

61. On the relationship between Marx and Keynes see, for example, L. Klein, *The Keynesian Revolution* (2nd edition) (London: 1966); P. Mattick, *Marx and Keynes* (London: 1971).

62. In fact, Wicksell was not translated until the 1930s – the *Lectures* in 1934 and *Interest and Prices* in 1936, although he did produce a summary of his ideas in the *Economic Journal* for 1907. Keynes's treatment of Wicksell in the *General Theory* is tantamount to ignoring him completely.

63. G. Myrdal's *Monetary Equilibrium* and E. Lindahl's *Studies in the Theory of Money and Capital* both appeared for the first time in English in 1939 (although they date from the late 1920s). A. P. Lerner reviewed them rather hostilely from a Keynesian standpoint in the *Canadian Journal of Economics and Political Science* (1939).

64. As with the case of Pigou, Keynes's treatment of Hawtrey, Lavington and Robertson was most inadequate.

65. J. R. (now Sir John) Hicks, 'Mr. Keynes and the Classics', *Econometrica*, V (1937). F. Modigliani, 'Liquidity Preference and the Theory of Interest and Money', *Econometrica*, XII (1944); D. Patinkin, *Money, Interest and Prices* (1st edition, 1956, 2nd edition, 1965).

66. See especially G. L. S. Shackle, 'Keynes and Today's Establishment in Economic Theory. A View', *Journal of Economic Literature*, Vol. XI (1973). Joan Robinson, 'The Second Crisis of Economic Theory', *American Economic Review*, Papers and Proceedings (May 1972).

67. See letter to J. R. Hicks, 31 March 1937, *Collected Writings of J. M. Keynes*, Vol. XIV, p. 79.

68. This is suggested by P. A. Samuelson in 'The General Theory', *Econometrica*, Vol. XIV (1946).

69. It is a usual presumption that the use of Keynesian policies would have lessened the burden of unemployment in the 1920s and 1930s. It cannot honestly be said however that this claim has been substantiated.

70. This dichotomy has affinities with the Kuhnian distinction

between paradigm change and changes within a paradigm.

71. Letter to R. F. Harrod, 27 August 1935, *Collected Writings*, Vol. XIII, p. 548.

72. H. G. Johnson, 'The Keynesian Revolution and the Monetarist Counter-Revolution', *American Economic Review*, Papers and Proceedings, May 1971.

## INTRODUCTION

*Professor W. Hagenbuch* (Chairman)

Sir Alec Cairncross is one of those splendid academics who has not only thought about economics and taught economics and published a steady stream of books and articles about how the economy works and how to make it work better, but has actually practised the art of economic management. He has spent half his long and productive career in the universities and half in government service. He has served on many official committees and Royal Commissions, too many to mention. He was economic adviser to Her Majesty's Government from 1961 to 1964 and head of the Government Economic Service from 1964 to 1969. He is now Master of St Peter's College, Oxford but continues to pour forth a steady stream of books and articles, to lecture, to sit on all sorts of committees and to promote economic wisdom in all quarters. He is a man of great experience, great wisdom and great commonsense, and this is a very rare combination indeed. We are very glad to welcome Sir Alec Cairncross, and I now call upon him to speak on the subject of 'Keynes and the Planned Economy'.

# KEYNES AND THE PLANNED ECONOMY

*Sir Alec Cairncross*

Keynesianism, said Richard Kahn recently, is in danger of becoming a dirty word. The mismanagement of the British economy is laid at Keynes's door long after his death. Was he not the man, in the words of Brendan Bracken, 'who made inflation respectable'? Who but Keynes is to be blamed for the 'mistaken' belief in budget deficits; in fine tuning; in a simplistic approach to demand management? Who turned our attention away from the quantity of money? Who killed the gold standard? Who destroyed belief in the good old automatic regulators and left us at the mercy of political misjudgement and cowardice? Above all, who opened the door to a steady growth of government intervention in economic affairs and with it an increasing invasion of individual rights and liberties?

It is a catechism that must sound curious to any economist brought up between the wars, when things were certainly different. It suggests a consistency and a weight of influence never attributed to Keynes in his lifetime. It overlooks Keynes's horror of inflation, his extensive writings on the subject, his warning (for it was his more than Lenin's) that to debauch the currency would prove the surest path to revolution and the destruction of capitalism. It represents Keynes of all people as an enthusiast for government intervention when almost the only government department for which he ever proposed new duties was the Treasury, a department with an administrative staff numbering just over twenty when he first joined it.

Similarly when the name of Keynes is associated with the idea of a 'planned economy' it is as well to remember how rarely the word 'plan' actually features in Keynes's writings. What he talks about constantly is *management*. The word appears in the heading to nearly every chapter of the *Treatise on Money*, Volume II, Book VII. In *The Means to Prosperity* there is again no reference to planning apart from a casual use of the word 'plan' in the Appendix. Policies, proposals, programmes, but no plans are discussed. The *General Theory* is equally silent on planning. It is only in *How to Pay for the War* that the word 'plan' is used over and over again to describe the proposals put forward. It is as if Keynes judged that economic policy in wartime has to be governed by fixed objectives that have no counterpart in normal peacetime operations and that while it may be appropriate to talk of 'economic management' when at peace, it is more appropriate to talk of 'planning' when at war.

Yet even when he used the term 'plan' Keynes did so in a very special way. The ideal type of plan in his view was the rule of the road. Nobody was the worse for having to conform to a general rule imposed from outside and the convenience of such a rule to all users of the road was conspicuous. Keynes thought the need to limit civilian demand in wartime an 'ideal opportunity for a common plan' satisfying the same criteria. Saving was a way of limiting demand but it was no good one man saving more if his neighbour promptly saved less. If all together saved more under a plan of deferred pay, demand could be kept within the limits required. The compulsions of planning for a predetermined goal became worthwhile because the alternatives – inflation on the one hand or shop shortages on the other – would distribute the same burden of economy between individuals more arbitrarily, less fairly and with more waste and more damage to the war effort. Only when there was an agreed objective beyond the reach of individual effort was there a case for planning.

The objectives of peacetime are less fixed than in wartime and the methods appropriate to their realisation have to be correspondingly more flexible. In this sense Keynes was the apostle of economic management rather than of economic planning. But the growth of economic management is largely a function of the more ambitious objectives that we now set for ourselves, partly under Keynes's influence: full employment, faster growth, greater economic equality, and so on.

If we ask what Keynes's contribution was to economic management as practised since the war we have to consider these objectives and how they appeared to Keynes and to those whom he influenced. We have to recognise that up to 1939 Keynes's direct influence on the system of economic management, although real, was limited and he could, of course, have no direct influence on the system as it has evolved since his death. When he re-entered government in the war his energies were heavily concentrated on external finance rather than domestic economic policy. His hopes were set on a better peacetime settlement than in 1919 and he was caught up in the prolonged international negotiations over postwar reconstruction. But since the volume of his collected works covering his activities in the Treasury during the Second World War has yet to appear, it is difficult to do justice to his contribution to thought and policy after 1939.

It seems best to start from what he himself had to say about the role of Government and then go on to review how far postwar developments reflect his ideas.

He was, of course, writing at a time when the state was a decidedly smaller element than now in the economic life of the country. Leaving aside defence expenditure and interest on the national debt, public expenditure had been under 6 per cent of GNP before the First World War and was about 14 per cent in the 1960s and a still higher percentage in the 1970s. If he was urging more action by governments it was not overloaded governments for whom he was prescribing.

Except for *The End of Laissez-Faire*, published 50 years ago, none of Keynes's writings provides us with a systematic analysis of the scope for government action. At no time in the last twenty years of his life did he publish a discussion of the economic functions of government. His interest in economic problems was largely a function of their urgency. In the 1930s, when unemployment was at its peak, it was the restoration of full employment that engaged him to the exclusion of lesser problems. In the last few years of his life he was concerned with the immediate problems of a war economy and the equally pressing need to prepare for the rebuilding of an international economy after the war. It was these problems that fuelled his imagination and were the starting-point of his theorising. He developed his theories in order to help him gain the right answers to urgent problems and to assist in persuading his colleagues that he had found the right answers.

Keynes moved from problems to analysis and from analysis to proposals for action without allowing his judgement to be inhibited by some preconceived view of the principles that should govern state intervention. Yet there is a consistent view of the state and its duties that emerges from his work and is given fullest and most coherent expression in *The End of*

*Laissez-Faire.*

There he quotes with approval Burke's dictum that 'one of the finest problems in legislation (is) to determine what the State ought to take upon itself to direct by the public wisdom, and what it ought to leave, with as little interference as possible, to individual exertion'.

'Perhaps', Keynes goes on, 'the chief task of economists at this hour is to distinguish afresh the *Agenda* of government from the *Non-Agenda*; and the companion task of politics is to devise forms of government within a democracy which shall be capable of accomplishing the *Agenda.*' In resorting to this Benthamite nomenclature Keynes emphasised that there could be no Benthamite presumption that government interference was 'generally needless' and 'generally pernicious'. His own view, which he frequently expressed, was that we were bound to settle for a mixed economy and that it was not possible to decide on abstract grounds what to include in the Agenda of government and what to exclude. He did however provide an important criterion of Agenda by suggesting the separation of those services which are technically social from those that are technically individual. 'The important thing for government', he argued, 'is not to do things which individuals are doing already, and to do them a little better or a little worse, but to do those things which at present are not done at all.'

He did not elaborate upon this important dictum but confined himself to three illustrations of it, covering a single page, and dealing in turn with control of credit, control of investment, and control of population. The first and most important is worth quoting in full:

> Many of the greatest economic evils of our time are the fruits of uncertainty, and ignorance. It is because particular individuals, fortunate in situation or in abilities, are able to take advantage of uncertainty and ignorance, and also because for the same reason big business is often a lottery, that great inequalities of wealth come about; and these same factors are also the cause of the unemployment of labour, or the disappointment of reasonable expectations, and of the impairment of efficiency and production. Yet the cure lies outside the operations of individuals; it may even be to the interest of individuals to aggravate the disease. I believe that

the cure for these things is partly to be sought in the deliberate control of the currency and of credit by a central institution, and partly in the collection and dissemination on a great scale of data relating to the business situation, including the full publicity, by law if necessary, of all business facts which it is useful to know. These measures would involve society in exercising directive intelligence through some appropriate organ of action over many of the inner intricacies of private business, yet it would leave private initiative and enterprise unhindered. Even if these measures prove insufficient, nevertheless, they will furnish us with better knowledge than we have now for taking the next step.

This passage is essentially a plea for demand management exercised through a central bank under public control or ownership. It is an idea that Keynes stuck to throughout his life, although his view of the causes of unemployment and business fluctuations changed and developed and he came to lay more weight on fiscal than on monetary policy in the exercise of management. The ingredients of the view are interesting. He starts off with risk, uncertainty and ignorance as the source of inequalities of wealth on the one hand and unemployment and inefficiency on the other. He then finds a remedy for ignorance in improved economic information and a way of neutralising risk and uncertainty through financial control over the economic conjuncture. He claims that this would permit of a reconciliation between the exercise of private initiative and the collective regulation of economic activity and so purge capitalism of some of its worst defects.

These are all recurrent themes in Keynes. He insisted on the need for improved data on economic aggregates. It was with his encouragement, as a believer in conjectural arithmetic, that Colin Clark and, later, James Meade and Richard Stone laid the basis for national income accounting. Any reader of *How to Pay for the War* must be struck by his efforts to make statistical bricks with very little straw; but in most of his earlier work one can find the same kind of calculations and the same appeal for more comprehensive and reliable statistics. Nothing would have pleased Keynes more than the transformation in economic statistics that has taken place in the past generation even if he might be chastened to find how much in the dark we remain about what is really going on in the economy.

In wanting more statistics did he want more state intervention? Not necessarily. He regarded more and better information as he regarded the rule of the road: something that helped everybody. Business needs better information just as much as government; and it also needs to learn how to use statistical information – a matter to which very little attention is customarily given.

It was also typical of Keynes to insist on the importance of risk and uncertainty. Keynes had given six years to the study of probability and a great many more to the study of the stock market. He was alive to the importance of luck, confidence, animal spirits and the state of mind of the business community. Investment, economic growth and the level of activity in the economy were all at the mercy of the unforeseen and of the confidence, or lack of it, with which the future was approached. Just as ignorance could be reduced by better information, risk and uncertainty could be reduced by better social organisation. Appropriate financial policies could moderate economic fluctuations and offer producers steadier and more calculable markets. It would be to the common advantage if the same output were produced with less ups and downs. It was a principle already familiar to pupils of Marshall and elaborated in Pigou's *Industrial Fluctuations.*

Then there is the 'appropriate organ of action', the central bank or Treasury, charged with the duty of eliminating fluctuations in activity. Here we have the key element in Keynes's approach to government activity. He was, *par excellence*, the Treasury man, the believer in financial agencies of control, who would regulate the economy by skilful management of demand rather than by interventions operating directly on supply. When the budget was small, as it was before the First World War, and when all orthodox opinion insisted that it should be balanced in peacetime, there was little or no scope for effective demand management through fiscal policy. So it was to monetary policy that Keynes looked for a regulator of demand in the 1920s and indeed until after the publication of the *Treatise*. It was only gradually that he came to see that the budget was a more comprehensive, direct and powerful 'organ of action' able to operate over the whole area of spending and saving, not just selectively like credit control. Monetary policy had proved too slow and too weak as a stimulant after 1932 and was likely to prove too expensive on the restrictive tack in wartime in terms of the interest burden it would leave behind. But there is no reason to suppose that Keynes was ever wedded to the one type of instrument rather than the other. What mattered was that control should be exercised over aggregate demand in the interests of full employment, less uncertainty and greater efficiency.

In all Keynes's writings we find the same insistence on monetary management as the prescription for a well-run economy. Throughout the interwar years it was as a monetary reformer that he was known and the proposals he put forward for consideration by government were invariably financial. At the outbreak of war when he came to write *How to Pay for the War* he again opted for a financial device. This time, however, it was not a device of monetary but of fiscal policy: deferred pay or postwar credits. He explained that it would not be possible to limit consumer demand sufficiently by high taxation and that the real choice lay between three possibilities: inflation; a system of postwar credits; and limitation of demand by shop-shortages mitigated by rationing. He regarded the latter course, just as he regarded inflation, as wasteful, inefficient and unjust. It would also detract from the war effort since it would involve running down stocks and deflecting supplies from exports and military requirements. But it was what we were heading for in the absence of a scheme of deferred pay.

Anyone who remembers these years will agree that Keynes was right to emphasise the importance of regulating effective demand, first by expanding it before the war and by keeping it within the limits of capacity thereafter. Much of the thinking of the period was hopelessly muddled because it started from supply, not demand, and relied on administrative controls over supply to bring back prosperity when these controls merely improved the position of one group compared with others. These were the days when quotas on Danish butter reduced the quantity imported but sent up the import bill; when unemployment was to be cured through land settlement; and when it seemed more important to some people to get prices up than output.

Even when Keynes felt that market forces were not working satisfactorily and would work better with government intervention, he thought instinctively of redirecting these forces rather than superseding them. For example, he was very much impressed by the instability of the commodity markets and the wide swings in the world price of primary commodities within extremely short periods. All this seemed to him highly inefficient and quite unnecessary. But his proposed remedy lay in a scheme for buffer stocks which would leave the commodity markets discharging their normal functions and allow the buffer stock manager to intervene freely and (if he did improve matters) profitably. Similarly when Keynes proposed limitation of imports in 1931 he suggested *not* the use of import quotas but a revenue tariff: a device less likely to cause disruption of normal market relationships, and similar in principle to the import surcharge introduced in 1964.

Nevertheless Keynes regarded various forms of intervention as indispensable to monetary management. It is difficult to say how far he was prepared to go in exercising control by limiting particular activities or constituents of total demand. He would certainly not have subscribed to the idea that it was sufficient to rely on control over the money supply especially if this meant that the monetary authorities should divest themselves of the whole panoply of monetary weapons that they had developed or contemplated. He was particularly insistent on the need to control investment, domestic and foreign, and was ready to support the use of quite sweeping powers for this purpose. So far as domestic investment was concerned he was conscious of the limitations of monetary weapons and accepted the need to vary public investment contracyclically through public works or in other ways. I doubt whether he would ever have favoured control of private *industrial* investment, but several times he urged the setting up of a National Investment Board to coordinate the larger schemes of capital development. Indeed, he would latterly have preferred limits on domestic investment by administrative action rather than by changes in credit conditions disturbing to accepted notions of the proper long-term rate of interest. Similarly, in face of the difficulty of reconciling full employment and external balance he wanted control over foreign investment and progressed from asking for control over new capital issues to insisting on the need for control over all outward movements of capital through exchange control. The full consequences (as well as the limitations) of such controls over investment were not apparent in

Keynes's lifetime.

In *The End of Laissez-Faire* Keynes outlined a second principle of government–industry relations supplementing the general argument for demand management. 'In many cases', he contended, 'the ideal size for the unit of control and organisation lies somewhere between the individual and the modern State.' 'I suggest', he went on, 'that progress lies in the growth and the recognition of semi-autonomous bodies within the State – bodies whose criterion of action within their own field is solely the public good as they understand it.'[1]

This idea by itself does not take us very far. Students of the behaviour of semi-autonomous bodies might want some guidance on the basis of identification of the public good. It is hard enough to lay down rules for the nationalised industries but a great deal harder to prescribe for semi-autonomous bodies that may want to know when and how far to bow to market forces, what customers to cater for or treat preferentially, how to balance the interests of employers, customers, owners, conservationists, minority groups and so on. The examples Keynes chooses – the universities, the Bank of England, and the Port of London Authority – do not bring out the nature of the problem that would be faced in productive industry if the only criterion of action were the public good.

It is also not at once clear what difference he has in mind between such a body and a nationalised industry. The distinction is not made easier to understand when he first hesitates over including the railway companies among semi-autonomous bodies and then argues that it would make very little difference if they were nationalised. 'There is', he says, 'no so-called important political question so really unimportant, so irrelevant to the reorganisation of the economic life of Great Britain, as the nationalisation of the railways.'[2]

What Keynes is really concerned to argue is that joint stock companies as they grow bigger and older come to behave more and more like public corporations. Writing 50 years ago – and what he says still applies – he pointed out that 'one of the most interesting and unnoticed developments of recent decades has been the tendency of big enterprise to socialise itself'.[3] I had always thought that I was making an original observation when I wrote after the war that British industry was semi-nationalised (especially when 75 per cent of industrial profits were paid in tax) and when I argued more recently that as the business unit grew larger and more monopolistic it became more and more indistinguishable from a public corporation.[4] But the gist of the matter is there already in 1926. Owners and managers grow apart: the making of large profits 'becomes quite secondary' while the stability and reputation of the business takes precedence; and all this is the more likely where its great size or semi-monopolistic position renders it 'conspicuous in the public eye and vulnerable to public attack'. Hence 'the battle of Socialism against unlimited private profit is being won in detail hour by hour'. On the other hand there is bound to be 'a waning of enterprise: the faults as well as the advantages of State Socialism'.

In spite of what he had to say about nationalisation of the railways, Keynes wanted public utility and other enterprises with large fixed capital requirements to be turned into public corporations. But he regarded the battle for greater public control of industry as largely phoney. Nineteenth century individualism and nineteenth-century state socialism sprang from the same intellectual root and were equally misguided: the one by a negative emphasis on avoiding limitations on freedom, the other by a positive stress on destroying monopoly. The task for the future 'must be to decentralise and devolve wherever we can, and in particular to establish semi-independent corporations and organs of administration to which duties of government, new and old, will be entrusted without, however, impairing the democratic principle or the ultimate sovereignty of Parliament'.[5]

Keynes's philosophy was nicely balanced between hatred of the love of money and hatred of bureaucracy and the muddle it caused. He was no admirer of unregenerate capitalism but declared that the *class* war would find him 'on the side of the educated *bourgeoisie*'.[6] He wanted more intervention in the interests of greater equality and yet not too much for fear of shackling freedom of private initiative. He would have liked a great redistribution of wealth through taxation, and proposed a capital levy, but recognised that if private enterprise were to function it would renew inequality by rewarding the lucky as well as the farsighted. To a remarkable degree he agonised far more over money than over power although others have felt it more repugnant to human dignity to acquiesce in the concentration of power than in the concentration of wealth. But he might well have echoed the comment of G. M. Young:

> People whose chief object in life is wealth are as a rule less intelligent than people whose object is power, but, on the other hand, are far less disposed to do active wrong to those beneath them or about them. They may, from negligence or selfishness or mere thick-wittedness, do much harm . . . but it is harm of a kind which is largely controllable by public opinion, by legislation, by science.[7]

A third important strand in Keynes's thinking – which, however, does not appear in *The End of Laissez-Faire* – was the need for international management. He was often accused of economic nationalism and in an anarchic world he accepted the need for each country to preserve its freedom of action. He wanted governments to begin by managing their own affairs: the domestic market, which they alone could regulate; the currency which reflected their own credit; the foreign exchanges, foreign lending and investment, and transactions with other countries. Without international management, however, the task of individual governments would become infinitely more difficult. Just as individuals could not develop their full potential without government planning of the level of effective demand and other matters, so individual countries would find it hard to keep in internal and external balance and maintain full employment unless they operated within a framework of international institutions planned and managed for the common good.

When Keynes started to develop this view in the 1920s there were practically no international institutions to build on apart from the League of Nations and occasional international conferences, none of them particularly successful. There was some cooperation between the most important central banks, especially between the Federal Reserve Board and the Bank of England. But the world financial system no longer danced to the tune of the Bank of England as it had done now and again in the nineteenth century. Even with the creation of the Bank of International Settlements in 1930 and the Tripartite Agreement between Britain, France and the United States in 1936 there was very little international management. It was only with the war that the possibility of creating an entirely new monetary system emerged. It was at this point that Keynes's personal influence was most strongly felt. What was finally agreed at Bretton Woods and after was not what he proposed but it did at least reflect much of his thinking.

It is hard for any young economist in 1976 to imagine the very different state of the world in, say, 1936. Nowhere is this more true than in the contrast in international institutions. One may lament the profusion of such institutions or their impotence or their philosophies. But they have at least one consequence that is often overlooked. They mean that the leading personalities in the economic life of the main countries know one another, are in frequent touch, and have had an opportunity to argue out their differences and compare notes on their successes and failures. This is true not only of the politicians who have always had opportunities of meeting but of senior administrators, business men and labour leaders whose horizons in the past were far more limited by national boundaries. International cooperation and planning may not yet be what Keynes had hoped for. But it is a great deal more real and more effective than in the years when he was trying to call it into being.

It is of course possible to take the view, as many people still do, that international management is a mirage, good for providing futile employment for thousands upon thousands of bureaucrats and diplomats, swelling the self-importance of governments as they stumble along the primrose path in pursuit of will-o'-the-wisps, and pandering to the popular illusion that governments and only governments have it in their power to change things for the better. There are those who sigh for automaticity, for the days of the gold standard, fixed exchange rates, and an inelastic money supply. They would rejoice if more things were taken out of the hands of governments and shaped by recognisable necessities. Those of this pessimistic school of thought distrust discretion in attempts to control what we only half understand. They would rather accept fixed rules to achieve fixed objectives, however harsh the consequences of abiding by the rules.

On this there is no doubt where Keynes stood. He trusted to human intelligence. He hated enslavement by rules. He wanted governments to have discretion and he wanted economists to come to their assistance in the exercise of that discretion. But he certainly held no exalted view of the wisdom of governments or the virtues of economic science. On the contrary he harped on the fallibility of governments and was for ever attacking the decisions they took. He was more charitable to his colleagues, the economists, but left the distinct impression in some quarters that until he came along they had spent much of their time preaching mistaken doctrines. No doubt he expected that in due course cries of '*tu quoque*' would be heard from his successors.

The unwisdom of governments and the errors of their advisers weighed less heavily with Keynes than the need to hold open the door to better management of our affairs. More damage would be done in the end by blind trust in some man-made institution that excluded all discretion than by considered policies which could improve through time as experience accumulated. In any event nearly all institutions did in practice leave room for discretion and those that did not were almost invariably modified so that they did. The gold standard, for example, was increasingly a managed standard. Equally, the rigid requirements of the Bank Charter Act of 1844, to take another example, had to be got round whenever they really began to bite. The choice is very, very rarely between management and some automatic rule dispensing with management; it is essentially between different ways of exercising managerial discretion and accepting or rejecting the need to consider well in advance where and how discretion might most fruitfully be called into play.

But of course Keynes never imagined that one can dispense with rules. Without them life is simply incalculable, arbitrary and chaotic. There has to be a framework of rules and conventions that one can take for granted and it is this framework that is described as a system. Keynes devoted himself in his last years to schemes for international monetary reform designed to create a new system that would harmonise international monetary relationships. The International Monetary Fund and the International Bank for Reconstruction and Development were not built to his specifications. But he recognised the need for institutions along those lines. The discretion that he wished national governments to enjoy had to be tempered by the discipline necessary for international collaboration and international management. What balance between the two he would now favour in the light of postwar experience no one can be sure; but it is certain that he would have wanted a system that would evolve, rules that could be altered as circumstances altered, and as much discretion as could be left to national governments consistently with the preservation of a satisfactory international system.

Given these strands in Keynes's thinking – demand management and control of investment in the interests of full employment; the potential development of public or semi-public corporations; and the need for a satisfactory international monetary system – what has Keynes's influence been on the policies of governments?

It was not very conspicuous before the war. He was listened to but his recommendations were rarely the basis of policy. When he published his *Essays in Persuasion* in 1931 he described them as 'the croakings of a Cassandra'. In the 1930s he gave his blessing to the cheap money policy pursued after the suspension of the gold standard but he was not the originator of the policy. Nor were his proposals for the finance of the war, although widely acclaimed, the cornerstone of budgetary policy. When deferred pay was introduced it was on a very limited scale: a gesture rather than Keynes's 'radical plan'. The capital levy that was to follow after the war never took place: when James Meade put it forward Keynes himself laughed the idea out of court as 'capital levity'. Family allowances, which he suggested in 1939, were introduced only when the war was over. The direction in which his influence was mainly felt before, during and after the war was in monetary policy and debt management. It was an influence exerted on the side of low rates of interest and a low burden of war debt. The consequences of this in the postwar period will be discussed in a moment.

After the war, when he was no longer alive to make his own contribution to policy, Keynes, in a sense, came into his own. His influence was exerted, as he had always expected, through a new generation in sympathy with his ideas. At the end of the *General Theory* he had pointed to the lag that usually attended the acceptance of new doctrines:[8]

> In the field of economic and political philosophy there are not many who are influenced by new theories after they are

25 or 30 years of age, so that the ideas which civil servants and politicians and even agitators apply to current events are not likely to be the newest.

By 1945, and still more by 1950, many of those who had been brought up on Keynes were well into their thirties and climbing into positions of influence in different countries. In the Central Banks and Ministries of Finance Keynesian ideas were sure of a hearing and increasingly accepted as a basis of policy. But in the process of elevation to an established ideology there was inevitably some oversimplification and a substitution of dogma for theoretical insight. Politicians in particular were content to know the endpoint to which Keynes's theories led without wasting time in tracing the path by which his conclusions were reached. There is a revealing passage in Ronald Walker's *From Economic Theory to Policy*, published in 1943, in which he describes how:[9]

> In the library of the Australian Parliament at Canberra there is a copy of the *General Theory*. The first 300 pages, in which the theory is worked out, are of virgin whiteness; the last 80 pages, with the practical applications, are well thumbed and heavily scored.

The idea that weighed most with politicians was that mass unemployment resulted from a deficiency of demand and could be cured by increased spending. This was not in itself a particularly helpful insight into the problems of the postwar world which proved to be very different from the world in which Keynes lived and wrote: a world in which unemployment stayed obstinately at an unprecedented level (never falling in the UK below two million in the 1930s) and in which it seemed inconceivable that prices could rise very much or very long in peacetime. In the postwar world, mass unemployment virtually disappeared and deflation was replaced by inflation. There was no lack of demand and rarely any governmental scruples about spending more for fear of unbalancing the budget.

One can regard this new situation in two ways. One can argue that the new generation of economic medicine men were equipped by Keynes to cure a disease that had disappeared and that their prescriptions for avoiding unemployment merely made inflation worse. Or one can argue that we owe it to Keynes that the problem of unemployment did not return after the war and that we have ourselves to blame if we have not worked out since his death how to combine full employment and stable prices.

Neither of these views seems to me satisfactory. Both attach far too much importance to the influence on events for good or bad of a particular set of ideas, which were by no means the exclusive basis of policy, if indeed policy had the importance in postwar economic development that both views assume. It seems to me very doubtful whether politicians are 'the slaves of some defunct economist', even if the economist is as powerful a thinker as Keynes; and still more doubtful whether in a democracy policies govern events rather than the other way round.

The universality of full employment in the postwar period, for example, makes it difficult to attribute it to successful economic management in a particular country or to the influence of Keynesian ideas in that country. It seems more likely that the circumstances were propitious for a prolonged investment boom and that the pressure for high government spending, although an important circumstance of this kind, was only vaguely connected with Keynesian ideas.

What was perhaps of more importance was the accommodating and often expansionary monetary policy pursued. Here there is a definite link with Keynes. In the early postwar years the British government in particular went out of its way to keep down the rate of interest. This was in its interest as a borrower and it was in the general interest of the taxpayer since the budget was correspondingly smaller. But it increased the incentive to invest when this was already strong and reinforced the inflationary pressures at work. Keynes might well have approved: the situation was quite unlike that in 1919–20 when he recommended putting the Bank Rate up to 10 per cent to curb a speculation boom. But if inflation was not to be controlled by monetary policy the alternative was to restrict consumption in other ways and continue control over investment. This was the policy which the government adopted.

It implied the use of physical controls of a kind that Keynes did not normally favour and a corresponding extension of government intervention in industry. It was not possible to control investment in the years immediately after the war merely by limiting capital issues, sending letters of guidance from the Bank of England to the commercial banks and similar devices. It was necessary to ration new building by an elaborate system of licensing and starting dates, complicated further by arrangements to allocate steel, timber, etc., and to limit investment in new plant by machinery licensing, including the licensing of individual machines procured from abroad. Some parts of the system were extraordinarily cumbersome and hopelessly inefficient: import licensing of machinery, for example, would have seemed to Keynes the prime example of a control to avoid. Similarly, control of international investment implied exchange control in great detail, often with the maximum inconvenience to businesses trading abroad; and it is not clear how far Keynes would have pressed for such control in face of the anomalies and frustrations it generated. What cannot be denied, however, is that by giving countenance to the idea of controlling investment, domestic and foreign, and insisting on low rates of interest in a potentially inflationary world, Keynes was throwing his weight behind a continuation of tight government control over industry and trade.

Although circumstances may have been favourable to full employment after the war the system of demand management that evolved to preserve it was undoubtedly Keynesian. This was particularly apparent in the technique of short-term economic forecasting that was developed. The whole system of thought underlying the forecasting derived from Keynes: the projection of effective demand by category, the interrelation between the constituent parts, the parameters, lags and mechanisms of adjustment, the emphasis on a limited horizon with more or less fixed resources, even the relegation of monetary influences (as distinct from expenditure influence) to a subordinate place. The Treasury was steeped in Keynes. But this was not true of other departments of government. The problems with which they wrestled did not disappear as soon as a steady pressure of demand was achieved. They were faced with the task of building things up, not of cutting things down to size, and on these positive tasks of organisation Keynes had little to say.

To put the matter concretely: what would Keynes have done in the Department of Economic Affairs or in the preparation of a National Plan? I think one can assume no enthusiasm for either. It is inconceivable that he could have encouraged the publication of anything called a 'plan' in a country on the verge of devaluation and not yet reconciled to it. But he was in any event strongly against planning in the sense of moulding an entire economy to meet fixed, detailed objectives specified without much regard to consumer demand.

Keynes did not survive the war long enough to take part in the postwar debate on planning. But he would have observed without surprise that the strongest commitment to planning was on the part of those with least experience of it, and that those who had spent the war in the planning of industrial outputs to meet government requirements (such as in the Planning Division of the Ministry of Aircraft Production) were the most sceptical of the pretensions of central planning. The great virtue of financial planning, in which Keynes did believe, was that it *de*centralised organisation while central planning did just the opposite. His kind of planning was intended to make possible an enlargement of individual freedom as the rule of the road does. So he found no difficulty in expressing agreement 'morally and philosophically' with 'virtually the whole' of Von Hayek's *The Road to Serfdom*, although he had some reservations about the pronouncements on economics.

'I should say', he wrote, 'that what we want is not no planning, or even less planning, indeed I should say that we almost certainly want more. But the planning should take place in a community in which as many people as possible, both leaders and followers, wholly share your own moral position.'[10]

Planning for Keynes meant regulating economic activity by demand management using fiscal and monetary policy. This involved more government intervention of a rather special kind: control over monetary policy, willingness to run budget surpluses and deficits, cooperation with other governments and international bodies like the IMF. But it did not necessarily imply an increase in the size of the budget or an extension of the public sector or intervention in the affairs of individual businesses or industries. It is not possible to regard full employment policy as responsible for any major enlargement of the role of the state or any positive encroachment on the freedom of the individual. On the contrary it was designed to give individuals the wider freedom that comes from the opportunity of employment. For this purpose all that Keynes required of the budget was that it should direct expenditure and raise revenue so as to redress any imbalance between the two in the private sector.

But if full employment is exonerated what is to blame for the heavier burdens we now put upon the state and for the harassments to which we expose ourselves in consequence? The answer is complex. On the one hand, there is the temper of the times. People have been increasingly predisposed to accept without challenge the need for government control to serve the common good. On the other hand there has been no lack of highly desirable aims for the government to profess. These aims have usually led the government to tax more and spend more and above all to administer more. It is fundamentally because we have set our sights higher and expect more from the state that it intervenes more in our lives.

One example of this is the call for greater economic equality. It is not easy to provide a simple measure of the amount of public expenditure to which this has given rise. But if we aggregate public spending in the United Kingdom on education, health and housing and add pensions and other social service benefits, the total comes to £28 600 million for 1975–6 or 60 per cent of total public expenditure, excluding debt interest. How much of this would be incurred if the ideas underlying the welfare state had never been formulated no one can say. But it is not unfair to regard this large total as reflecting an endeavour to ensure some minimum standard of provision for all and the bulk of it as a transfer from the better-off to the less well-off.

The budgetary consequences, however, are only part of the story. In all kinds of ways legislation conceived in the interests of equality, fairness and non-discrimination complicates the life of us all. The National Health Service is a good example. Expenditure has grown steadily because unless it expands it is necessary to deny treatment to some while granting it to others and at the same time the progress of medical science makes the treatment of each progressively more expensive. Once medical services have to be rationed – as a ceiling on expenditure would dictate – queues necessarily form and issues of parity of treatment begin to assume more importance and occupy more time.

Equality, moreover, is only a single strand in government intervention. There is also the effort to promote faster economic growth. With no Keynes to reveal the secret of faster growth, the state is the more determined to take action the less successful its previous efforts. It is ambitious to demonstrate its success in the latest and most expensive products of technology, rushing in with unlimited funds where private investors are inevitably and justifiably more cautious. The state becomes increasingly interventionist because it is increasingly fidgety and dissatisfied with the pace set by private industry.

Thus it is not possible to lay at Keynes's door responsibility for the great extension in the part the state plays in our life. As I have explained elsewhere,[11] the origins of this lie in forces more powerful than the vision of even the greatest of social scientists: in the aftermath of two world wars that mobilised the entire population under the banner of the nation-state; the transfer of power to the manual worker that this involved; the growing realisation of that power under conditions of full employment and the perception that it could be used through the state for economic and social ends; the spread of democratic ideals by which the transfer of power was legitimised; the development of the welfare state and steeply progressive taxation as the outcome of these ideals; and on top of these political trends the steady pressure of a centralising technology in industry and government and the emergence of a powerful and competent bureaucracy in response to that pressure.

The dominant forces at work making for increased state intervention were not let loose by Keynes nor would they have enjoyed his unqualified approval. Yet in one important way they gained strength from his influence and his ideas. For the centralising tendencies would have been greatly weakened in the absence of a fuller understanding of economic management such as Keynes helped to supply. It was a sense of improved understanding that emboldened the state to extend its responsibilities: a belief that Keynes had liberated us from ignorance and danger so that economic forces would never again be allowed to get out of hand. Indeed, since regulation by the state was inevitable if full employment was to be secured, the more deeply the state involved itself in the running of the economic system the better.

Against this must be set the really important contribution that Keynes would have claimed he was making to our conception of how an economy should be run. For him 'the commanding heights of the economy' were not this industry or that. He had no use for an extensive programme of nationalisation nor for elaborate schemes of licensing and control. What mattered was control of *demand*; and this could be exercised quite simply through existing financial machinery by the Treasury and the Bank of England. He wanted the *minimum* of intervention consistent with the fullest sustainable use of the country's resources. He should be credited with the retreat from the attempt after the war to perpetuate wartime controls by christening them 'planning' rather than charged with the subsequent outbreaks of interventionism, under banners no less misleading. Keynes taught us how to plan through the budget. There *are* other ways of planning. But those who think they understand them would do well to make sure before advocating them that they have first grasped the full significance of Keynes's approach to planning.

Keynes insisted on control over the level of effective demand as a precondition of full employment. But he was well aware that this was not a sufficient condition. His writings in the 1930s are strewn with references to perversities in the behaviour of markets that might thwart the efforts of governments to expand demand: panic reactions based on slogans of the past or distrust of governmental intentions. Deficit financing, for example, might be ineffective in a world in which business retrenched still more in face of what it took to be evidence of unsustainable extravagance by governments. Attempts to create additional liquidity by adding to the money supply might merely generate alarm and an appetite for still more liquidity or lead to an outflow of funds and pressure on the foreign exchanges. Demand management might not be the straightforward business it is so often thought to be.

But there was also a much bigger reservation to be made. Keynes saw earlier and more clearly than most other economists that curing unemployment would weaken the economy's resistance to the inflationary bug. In the *Economic Journal* in 1943[12] he referred to the view that:

> a capitalist country is doomed to failure because it will be found impossible in conditions of full employment to prevent a progressive increase of wages. According to this view severe slumps and recurrent periods of unemployment have

been hitherto the only effective means of holding efficiency wages within a reasonably stable range. Whether this is so or not remains to be seen. The more conscious we are of this problem, the likelier we are to surmount it.

Writing to Frank Graham at the end of 1943 he asked:[13]

> How much otherwise unavoidable unemployment do you propose to bring about in order to keep the Trade Unions in order? Do you think it will be politically possible when they understand what you are up to?

He went on to argue that 'other, more reasonable, less punitive means must be found'. But he did not claim to have found them. To another correspondent at the end of 1943 he wrote:

> The task of keeping efficiency wages reasonably stable (I am sure they will creep up steadily in spite of our best efforts) is a *political* rather than an economic problem.[14]

And in June 1945 he was writing:

> One is also, simply because one knows no solution, inclined to turn a blind eye to the wages problem in a full employment economy.[15]

But how can one go on turning a blind eye? One has to decide whether the labour market responds to the money supply or *vice versa.* If wage inflation is essentially a political problem how can we be sure that the Keynesian prescription for full employment would not call for extensive government intervention? The prescription calls for political action to prevent wages from rising ahead of productivity and we do not know what political action would be required in order to do what unemployment is alleged to have done in the past to temper the bargaining power of labour to the needs of price stability. So long as we do not know we cannot say with assurance how much intervention and what kinds of intervention Keynes would have accepted as the price of full employment.

NOTES

1. 'The End of Laissez-Faire', *Essays in Persuasion, Collected Writings*, Vol. IX, p. 288.

2. Ibid., p. 290.

3. Ibid., p. 289.

4. *The Market and the State*, ed. Thomas Wilson and Andrew S. Skinner, (Oxford: 1976), p. 126.

5. 'Am I a Liberal?', *Essays in Persuasion*, *Collected Writings*, Vol. IX, p. 302.

6. Ibid., p. 297.

7. G. M. Young, *Sunday Times* (14 January 1940).

8. *General Theory of Employment, Interest and Money*, pp. 383–4.

9. E. R. Walker, *From Economic Theory to Policy* (University of Chicago Press: 1943), p. 72.

10. Cited by R. F. Harrod, *The Life of John Maynard Keynes* (London: 1951), p. 436.

11. *The Market and the State*, op. cit., p. 128 *et seq.*

12. Keynes, *Economic Journal* (June–September 1943), pp. 183 and 185, quoted by Lord Kahn in 'On Re-reading Keynes', *Proceedings of the British Academy*, Vol. LX (1974), p. 379.

13. Lord Kahn, loc. cit., p. 380.

14. Ibid., p. 387.

15. Ibid., p. 387.

## DISCUSSION

*Sir Austin Robinson:* We have had two splendid talks and I have enjoyed them enormously. May I be allowed to harp back to Bernard Corry, with whom I find myself disagreeing to a greater extent than I do with Sir Alec Cairncross? But may I first be allowed to add one other anniversary to those that were marked at the beginning? It is just 30 years this year since Keynes died. There are very few of us who will ever be remembered 30 years after we have died, and it is extraordinary that the centre of economics should still be about Keynes, 30 years after he died. But what I would particularly like to say a word or two about is what Bernard Corry was saying about Keynes's attacks on the classical economics, because I believe that he has missed the true target.

I am delighted that Bernard Corry has brought us back to the problems of Pigou and Dennis Robertson. I had very much hoped that now that we have been able to publish Volumes XIII and XIV of Keynes's *Collected Writings* people would have soaked themselves in them. But I hope that you will at the same time remember that there was a tremendous amount of argument going on in Cambridge in the 1930s which never got onto bits of paper, and so cannot be printed and recorded for you. And please remember that we had in Cambridge – as Sir Alec Cairncross will bear out – the ablest lot of undergraduates and postgraduates that I ever remember having had in Cambridge together at one time. And a great deal of the argument was going on with them. So that if you are trying to rehabilitate Pigou, please be prepared to go through as tough a job of thinking and analysis as that group went through in Cambridge. You are not going to be able to do this by hasty reading and dashing off some conclusions. You have got to be prepared to do some really very hard work indeed if you are going to do anything serious. May I add just by way of clarification that Taussig was very much read in Cambridge. It was the first book I was ever given to read myself in the field of economics.

But I was saying that I think that Bernard Corry has missed the target. The person that Keynes was really gunning for was not Pigou; it was Keynes himself. Keynes had lectured down to 1914. He had given the basic lectures on monetary theory. He knew what he had said, but those lectures had not been published and he could not document his disagreements with classical economics as it was interpreted in Cambridge at that period by referring to what he had said in his own lectures. I had myself for a year or two tried, from 1923, to give the monetary lectures; I know what I was saying at that time; I know that what I was saying at that time was what I, at any rate, ten years later would have regarded as nonsense. Thus Keynes was gunning for himself. But he had to document the discarded points of view, and he documented by drawing on Pigou. I am sorry for Pigou, and if Bernard Corry can persuade us, or if his very able research students can persuade us, that there was more to be said for Pigou than has been said, I could not be more delighted.

But what I want to do for one moment is to go back to 1920 in Cambridge. That was the year in which I started trying to learn economics. I went to lectures by Pigou on value theory in the Arts School in Cambridge. I then got on a bicycle and bicycled right across Cambridge to Hubert Henderson lecturing on monetary theory. I then got on a bicycle again and bicycled across to Emmanuel College and listened to Lavington lecturing on industrial fluctuations. These were then three entirely different subjects which were in no way connected with each other and which, in Cambridge at any rate in those days, had not been in any proper sense integrated together. What I felt a few years later was coming out of the early thinking, partly of Dennis Robertson in *Banking Policy and the Price Level*, partly in Keynes's *Treatise*, but more than ever in the *General Theory*, was an integration of these subjects. I suffer, I am sure, from *anno domini*; but I find it extraordinarily difficult to see how some of the monetary theorists today are really integrating and reconciling the whole concept of the formation of prices with their ideas of monetary theory. That was the problem with which we were wrestling in the 1930s.

I would just like to add, because it has a relevance to this, that Don Patinkin organised a conference in Canada last October on the subject of the Cambridge origins of Keynesian economics. It was an extremely interesting conference. The papers and the discussions, edited by Don Patinkin, will be published by Macmillan in a few months time. You will see where we were getting at that conference in regard to some of the problems we are discussing today.

May I say finally how interested I was by Bernard Corry asking what seems to me the fundamental question? If you have something in economics that you think it is extraordinarily important to persuade the rest of the world about, do you do it by writing an article which everybody is going to read and pass over in the *Economic Journal*? Do you leave the people concerned to see how they might conceivably modify their current models of thinking? Or do you go bald-headed at them and try to emphasise the differences? I believe Keynes was right to emphasise the differences rather than the minor progressions. I get a little lost when Bernard Corry talks about the old guard keeping up its resistance to these new ideas. I find it very difficult to understand how you know whether somebody has changed or not changed. I know that Ralph Hawtrey never changed his model of discussing monetary theory. I know that Fritz Hayek never changed his model of thinking. I am a lot less certain that Theodore Gregory did not move a lot as the years went on. I know that Lionel Robbins moved a lot as years went on. But I think the real test here is not what they first said about the *General Theory*, but the way they wrote and the way they analysed their own problems from then on. And I think you will find that there are many more people who *absorbed* the essentials of the Keynesian revolution, if one calls it that, than ever said so on paper.

*Mr Kemp:* I studied my economics at the Henry George School, not at university. I'd like to ask the question: what is the state of thinking among Keynesian economists today on the actual evidence for the mismatch, or supposed mismatch, between saving and investment? What is the theoretical and what is the statistical evidence to support the contention? And how in fact can it in the end be supported so long as, for example, banks are willing to accept deposits from individuals and offer interest even at minimal rates?

*Professor Corry:* I'm not sure I can answer that. It does, however, come back to the point I was making in my talk about new ideas in economics; that is, we seem to demand theoretical revolutions. You would think, wouldn't you, that before the *General Theory* was accepted there would have been a refutation of other models – an empirical refutation – and that we would not have accepted the new ideas until they had been backed up with evidence? But for various reasons economics doesn't seem to go like that. It is a fact though isn't it, to go back to your question, that practically overnight economists accepted the idea that there wasn't an automatic regulator between savings and investment, and most economists today would accept that position? If you ask me what is the empirical evidence, I'll have to confess it's not clear.

But if I can just mention an analogy. We've been assuming – because I didn't want to get into yet another difficult area – that there is clear evidence that Keynesian measures in the early 1930s would have 'improved the situation', but I'm not sure that we have got good econometric evidence for that period showing us the different tradeoffs between unemployment and inflation, and between unemployment and the balance of payments. Indeed the recent work by some young economic historians is now doubting the built-in assumption that Keynesian measures would have 'improved the situation'.

*Professor Kennedy:* I'd like to ask Bernard Corry about this view that Keynes was insisting on a theoretical revolution rather than on a policy revolution. As far as I understood there has been some correspondence which has come to light, I think with Hicks, in which Hicks wanted to qualify some of Keynes's theoretical points and Keynes wrote back 'I know that but I couldn't develop that because I had to make the theory as simple as I possibly could in order to get the policy conclusions across'. So that I would have thought there was a case for thinking that it was the policy revolution that Keynes was mainly concerned with.

*Professor Corry:* Yes, obviously he wanted to change policy; I don't think that is inconsistent with the view that I've put. When dealing with civil servants or Commissions he was mainly concerned with policy. But it is quite clear in his correspondence, particularly with Dennis Robertson and with Sir Roy Harrod, that he wanted to convince them of the theoretical basis of his policy recommendations. He may have been operating differently with the academic group than with the 'Whitehall group', but his insistence on a theoretical revolution comes out quite clearly I think in his correspondence with Dennis Robertson because Robertson kept saying to him 'look I agree about public works', and Keynes said 'that's not enough, I want commitment to my theoretical ideas'.

*Professor Hutchinson:* I would like to agree with about 85 or even 90 per cent of Professor Corry's paper, including what he said about Pigou, and what he has just said about the stress on theory rather than on policy. Regarding Pigou, one must remember that Keynes himself said in 1937 – it's in Vol. XIV of the *Collected Writings*, I think – 'on practical policy matters there is extremely little between us'. Pigou had signed the same sort of letters to *The Times* in the early 1930s on the desirability of public works. So I agree with Professor Corry on all that. I disagree with him, however, about the earlier classicals; that the whole idea of classical economics from the start was a Keynesian myth. You can't get much more classical than Smith and Ricardo, and they were very consistent upholders of a classical (in the Keynesian sense) model right across the board and with its implications for policy. What came to be called the Treasury view in 1929 should be called the Ricardian view. It had been proclaimed in parliament by Ricardo in 1819; and it achieved great influence throughout the nineteenth century. It's quite true that John Stuart Mill is a bit ambivalent, as in many other matters, but there was a very powerful classical view. It only began to disintegrate in a very unsystematic way about 50 years before the *General Theory*. In other words, I would say that the Keynesian view of the history of economic thought is very good in its earlier part. It goes wrong about his contemporaries. That's like the Marxian version of the history of economic thought. Marx was a great scholar of the history of economic thought, but he goes wrong about his contemporaries because he wanted to show that he was the one scientific disinterested economist. Keynes had great insights but he was apt to go wrong about his contemporaries.

*Sir Austin Robinson:* I think it's complete nonsense to ask either/or about whether Keynes was interested in theory or policy. He was interested in both. Surely his great contribution to economics was to see a policy problem and then to see the theoretical implications of trying to solve it. The two things, I'm perfectly certain, to Keynes went always hand in hand and one mustn't ask whether he was interested in one or the other.

*Mr Oksuz:* I have a question for Sir Alec Cairncross. If I listened to him correctly he said that Keynes thought the causes of our predicaments were uncertainty, risk and ignorance. Did Keynes think that these problems could be mitigated by appropriate budgetary policy and, if so, are our present predicaments the result of bad budgeting or the result of other factors that Keynes did not foresee?

*Sir Alec Cairncross:* I don't think it was in Keynes's mind that reducing risk and ignorance was primarily a matter for the budget. When he talked about uncertainty and ignorance he was thinking of investment, and the long horizon that entrepreneurs have to have in coming to decisions about investment policy. He laid stress on better information, and I don't think that anybody who is brought up today has any understanding of what it was like in a period when there were no figures of GNP, no figures of the balance of payments, no figures on almost any economic aggregate that we are now accustomed to reading daily on the front page of the newspaper. The front pages of newspapers had never heard of these things when I started economics, let alone gave you figures to measure them. Keynes was indicating that if you are trying to form a judgement of the future you must have information that allows you to see what the trends are, to form a view about what the future is likely to be. Keynes's essential interest was in reducing ignorance about the future to a minimum by providing the fullest possible information for judgement.

*Dr Nabiel:* I would like to comment briefly on the so-called Keynesian revolution referred to in both the development of economic theory and economic policy. Firstly, on the question of economic theory – or perhaps a more suitable term would be economic ideology – Professor Corry, in my view, was right in his remark that if one looks at the standard macroeconomics textbook it usually starts from a chapter on the classical theory and then it moves on to Keynes and his theory. The way these textbooks are structured gives the impression, and leads many students to believe, that what can be defined as Keynesianism was the product of a single person; a scientific breakthrough being the result of a discovery by a genius and representing a completely new stage in the development of economic thought. In some ways this myth is reflected in the fashionable term 'Keynesian Revolution'.

Keynes's contribution to economic theory can be evaluated properly only if seen in the context of the times in which he lived and the whole preceding period of reassessment and revision of the classical principles and dogmas. I would like to refer, for example, to Klein's book *The Keynesian Revolution* which in an interesting and profound way analyses the discussions which had been going on after the First World War and which led gradually to the erosion of the foundations of the classical concept as the *modus operandi* of the capitalist economy. The theoretical conclusion that Keynes reached in the *General Theory* should be rather seen as the culmination of those discussions, and this by no means implies a diminution of Keynes's own original contribution. May I add that Klein's book would have been of greater value if he had not concentrated on the Anglo-Saxon world only but had also taken into account the discussions which had taken place in Germany, for example, in which Ludwig Von Mises was so prominent.

On the question of the so-called Keynesian Revolution in economic policy, what Keynes tried to accomplish in the *General Theory* was to build up a consistent and coherent general equilibrium model and to show that there is an objective need for a modern economy to be managed in order to achieve full employment. Whatever part of the model we take, be it wage determination, aggregate consumption or investment, or the rate of interest, the analysis of all those components in his model is based on a number of simplifying assumptions which, as a method of analysis, is unavoidable. In the light of further developments of economic theory one may argue about the validity of various assumptions or conclusions reached by Keynes; some of them in the course of time have been developed, others rejected. But all this does not undermine the relevance of the central message passed on to us by Keynes, namely that a modern economy, in order to achieve fundamental goals of economic policy, needs to be managed and needs an overall strategy and that this task should be the responsibility of a government. This is the quintessence of the Keynesian policy revolution.

# KEYNES AND PLANNING
*Lord Balogh*

Those of us who served with Sir Alec Cairncross in the Civil Service will savour his paper on 'Keynes and the Planned Economy' as the sort of gem which we can expect from him. It starts with a series of rhetorical questions – not of course reflecting Sir Alec's views but those of an ultra-liberal monetarist – about Keynes's impact on the world economy and implying his responsibility for all the ills of the world and obviously inviting the word 'num' at the beginning. It is the last and most absurd of these questions which Sir Alec characteristically chooses for his own reply. This equates Keynes with state intervention and planning, and thus with the loss of liberty: 'Above all, who opened the door to a steady growth of government intervention in economic affairs and with it an increasing invasion of individual rights and liberties?'

To me it seems idle to speculate about the views of great men some generation and a half or so after their death. So much has happened that was hardly foreseeable; so many harsh lessons were taught but often not learned. And in the case of Keynes, moreover, there was his infinite pliancy, his wonderful response to intelligent stimulus. Without knowing who his friends would be now – the Treasury? His old Cambridge acolytes and inspirers? His prewar opponents? – how would it be possible to divine what would be his attitude? His strength and infinite, yet tantalising, charm lay in being able to discard views (and people) at the drop of a hat.

Yet I can see very good reason indeed for Sir Alec's choice. Sir Alec is evidently engaged on a vital rescue operation essential if Keynes's great authority and name are not to be wickedly appropriated by those who believe that *some* measure of planning and *some* direct controls are needed if full employment and stability are to be combined under a democratic system of government.

The reaction of the profession to the dead Keynes was at first unquestioning apotheosis. This phase lasted some twenty years between 1946–66 (or was it 1968?). Fine tuning of demand was the ultimate answer to the pre-Second World War woes. As the title of Arthur Okun's book *The Political Economy of Prosperity*[1] indicates, a new 'science' had been born; the doubts generated by the Great Depression had been made to vanish for ever. Keynes, the sorcerer, had triumphed.

There was a snag: inflation. It turned out to be a fatal one. Just as the neoclassical economics foundered on the contrast between the colossal wartime employment and output and the misery of the 1930s and on its inability to deal with the problem of business cycles (that awkward 'unexplained residue' for which 'pure equilibrium theory . . . (cannot) provide any explanation'),[2] so the Keynesian liberals were unable to explain or deal with the general tendency to inflation which has undermined governments and threatened the very structure of society.

The new 'science' also seemed sterile, although the period of its prominence was far more prosperous and secured far higher employment levels than any preceeding period. The Phillips curve apparently provided proof that full employment and price stability could be reconciled. Unfortunately, for the liberal (conservative) Keynesian, however, this curve vanished at the end of the 1960s (if it ever existed).

The failure of Keynesian policies in containing inflation has unfortunately not led to a reconsideration in a Keynesian spirit of the policy means needed. This Keynesian spirit was well expressed by him as long ago as 1925: a policy which tries to control prices and wages by monetary restriction 'by intensifying unemployment without limit . . . is a policy . . . from which any humane or judicious person must shrink'.[3]

Instead, what happened was the revivification of the discredited monetarist school based on the quantity theory of money, and the rise of a rival new empirical school in Cambridge. The latter accepted the monetarist view that fine tuning is at least in practice destabilising, and attributed balance of payments crises to an overblown public sector borrowing requirement, upsetting an otherwise stable system.

Both schools, however distant their starting points, agreed that state intervention created unbalance. On the remedy, however, they disagreed. What was needed, according to the monetarists, was a steady increase in the volume of money neither more nor less than the rate of increase of productivity in the system (shades of the previous *nostrum*: demand should be kept at a level neither lower nor higher than that corresponding to the full employment of resources). The monetarists did not give any explanation of how the changes in the volume of money would be translated into expenditure. Yet even their basic foundation, the quantity 'equation' $MV = PT$, was fraught with unexplained methodological difficulties. As it stood it was, of course, no more than an identity unusable for policy advice. It was transformed into an equation by a number of unproven assumptions or rather claims about the significance and the behaviour of each of the components. Thus it was assumed that $V$ (the velocity of circulation of money) was constant; that $T$ (the volume of transactions) was determined by the real resources available arranged in a Walrasian balance, and that $P$ (prices) were the passive entity reacting to changes in the active variable $M$ (the volume of money). Unfortunately $V$ and $T$ could not be ascertained directly. Thus a dummy ratio of national income to monetary circulation was substituted as a measure of the velocity of circulation, and for transactions, national income was substituted. The use of these 'proxies', however, and indeed of the definition of $M$ itself, is most questionable. Where do liquid assets end and money begin? Which of the short-term assets should be included was arbitrary and debatable.[4]

The vast differences between $M_1$ (cash) and $M_3$ (cash plus (some) deposits) show the importance of the choice, especially as the latter includes a sizeable proportion of the formers' transactions velocity of circulation. A further anomaly is that the dummy for $T$ excludes all non-income transactions (house purchases, other transfers of assets, realisation of paper profits etc.), while the definitions of money include all relevant assets belonging to the *non-personal* private sector. It has not been demonstrated – and is very questionable – that the motivations of giant firms in holding cash and/or increasing their other assets are similar to those of wage and salary earners; that is, that the national income is an adequate dummy for total transactions. The true velocity of circulation is not merely much higher but also more unstable than the income velocity, and its variations under the impact of changed psychology are probably an important source of economic fluctuations. But even in the case of the latter there is much doubt about Friedman's statistical 'proofs'.[5] Changes in stocks, such as of inert deposits, are not caught. Neither are capital gains which subsequently appear in incomes. Why a single number indicator should reflect all complicated transactions (for example, the speculative excesses of financiers) dislocating the system, has not been disclosed. The monetarists, moreover, operate on the basis of a Walrasian model. The growth of oligopoly which was appreciable in the US and rapid in the UK is dismissed. For example the ubiquitous Harry Johnson asserts rather wildly:[6] This (the imperfect-monopolistic competition) revolution has more or less fizzled out, though its fossilised remains continue to plague both students and their instructors in elementary courses'. Yet even Professor (now Sir John) Hicks admitted in his Nobel-prizewinning volume:[7]

> It is, I believe, only possible to save anything from this wreck – and it must be remembered that the threatened wreckage is that of the greater part of economic theory – if we can assume that the markets confronting most of the firms with which we shall be dealing do not differ very greatly from perfectly competitive markets. If we can suppose that the percentages by which prices exceed marginal costs *are variable*, and if we can suppose (what is largely a consequence) that marginal costs do generally increase with output at the point of equilibrium (diminishing marginal costs being rare), then the laws of an economic system working under perfect competition will not be appreciably varied in a system which contains widespread elements of monopoly. At least, this getaway seems well worth trying. We must be aware, however, that we are taking a dangerous step, and probably limiting to a serious extent the problems with which our subsequent analysis will be fitted to deal.

Friedman in a cavalier way disregards these difficulties. He at least implicitly accepts a model in which there are so many (small) units (including wage-earners) that they are unable to influence prices (including wages) as in a Walrasian system of perfect competition:[8]

> The natural rate of unemployment . . . is the level that would

be ground out by the Walrasian system of general equilibrium equations, provided there is embedded in them the actual structural characteristics of the labour and commodity markets, including market imperfections, stochastic variability in demands and supplies, the cost of gathering information about job vacancies and labour availabilities, the cost of mobility, and so on.

This formulation tries to escape the awkwardness posed by bilateral monopoly and growing oligopoly and by the importance of increasing returns in the markets for goods and services, by 'absorbing' these difficulties (rather like the way 'free trade' authors dealing with foreign trade or growth 'absorb' them). Unfortunately for this 'school', this acceptance, in fact, precludes the 'grinding out' of determinate answers. There is a further snag. The Walrasian model is strictly static; that is, it presupposes perfect foresight. This is not likely to be useful in explaining contemporary events such as business fluctuations. The monetarists therefore thought that they could make it relevant (as if the assumption of perfect competition does not itself rule it out of the running) by adopting a new gimmick, the 'REH' (as in-group Chicagoans call it) *or* rational expectations hypothesis. Its relevance can be best demontrated by trying to describe it: 'rational economic agents will endeavour to form expectations of relevant future variables by making the most efficient use of all information provided by past history'.[9] This, the monetarists claim, is sufficient for rendering all state intervention *a priori* harmful. Looking at the extreme fluctuations of the stock and commodity markets as well as of investment one is not inclined to accept this further refinement of the discredited neoclassical microeconomic faith.

The 'new' Cambridge school dodged the issue. It condemned short-term forecasts, but did not vouchsafe rules by which they could be avoided when building up a longer-run prediction.

These considerations suggest that the idea that a modern economic system is inherently stable is without the slightest foundation. Kaldor, as far back as 1940, has put forward a model which being open-ended can explain why even random shocks should cause self-perpetuating fluctuations.[10]

The thrust of my argument is, then, that neither of these liberal or liberal-type approaches are able to form the basis of a successful policy against inflation. Sir Alec's argument does not go into this remarkable failure. He argues:

> The universality of full employment in the postwar period, for example, makes it difficult to attribute it to successful economic management in a particular country or to the influence of Keynesian ideas in that country. It seems more likely that the circumstances were propitious for a prolonged investment boom and that the pressure for high government spending, although an important circumstance of this kind, was only vaguely connected with Keynesian ideas.

This ignores the immense increase in public expenditure, particularly on arms ('digging holes and filling them up again'), and the decisive influence of foreign (Marshall) aid and the suspension of all restrictive rules forced upon the world (and more especially Britain) which had been outlawed by the American *Diktat* at Bretton Woods. Sir Alec also ignores the fact that it can hardly be a coincidence that with the revival and increasing influence in leading countries of the monetarist teaching, mass unemployment has returned and with it the view that government intervention has always had a destabilising effect. This has been claimed by Professor Musgrave in the Brookings Report on Britain[11] and lately, as we have seen, by the new Cambridge School.[12] It had been much earlier and more tentatively suggested by Christopher Dow's analysis in his *The Management of the British Economy 1945–1960.* I think that the methodology of the econometric exercise used in the Brookings Institution volume has been very effectively criticised by David Worswick in his contribution to *Britain's Economic Prospects Reconsidered*, edited by Sir Alec Cairncross, and I will not try to repeat it.

So far as the new Cambridge School is concerned, I showed some scepticism at its birth about what I felt was the subtle transformation of an identity *ex post*, into a strategic equation *ex ante*, a procedure which cost us so much unnecessary difficulty in connection with the savings/investment identity during the prewar disputes about the *General Theory*. I note just in passing that Mr Godley's model was based on an empirical relationship without logical explanation. It was, moreover, so constructed that by definition it is the state's intervention, and, more especially, the surplus and deficit in the Budget, which could cause destabilisation of the system, with other changes, including the volume of exports and value of imports, being smoothly harmonised.

I should have thought that experience with the so-called Phillips curve would have warned economists about the dangers implicit in the building of elaborate theories on ephemeral empirical relations. This new 'law' like many others did not remain long in force (if it ever was). Even if the econometrics or the theoretical methodology of these efforts had been correct, the question itself, whether government intervention was destabilising, was, in my opinion, not meaningful and consequently no econometric results could be relevant. This follows from the analysis of a century of business cycles in Professor Pigou's monumental work, *Industrial Fluctuations*,[13] and from Nicholas Kaldor's 'Model of the Trade Cycle'.[14] In both theories the unavoidable alternations of cumulative and psychologically induced upward and downward movements, exacerbated by the irrepressible elasticity of the monetary system, are responsible for the extent of the fluctuations (though in the Kaldor model some interesting and open-ended features are incorporated which contribute to the fluctuations). The all-important conclusion is that an economy based on individual decision-making is inherently unstable.

Even if the postwar stop–go cycles up to 1973–74 were far less violent than the prewar ones, it is difficult to avoid the conclusion that the former were different only in degree and not in kind from those of the latter. That difference was caused mainly by the vast increase in the importance of the public sector combined with the strong upward pressure on costs and prices by the greater strength of trade unions.

The inescapable lesson of the pre-Second World War cycles (and the post-1972 boom and bust) is that all indirect policy measures, whether monetary or fiscal, can operate only through their psychological impact. But this necessitates 'overkill'; that is, measures are required to be more savage than is indicated by the 'objective' needs of full employment once the 'boom' has broken (or vice versa).

Since 1943, I have held that only direct controls and a pervasive voluntary agreement on incomes could harmonise full(ish) employment and stability. Without them the system would experience upward pressure which in the end would lead to a monetary explosion or a reversal of the cumulative upward movement – and this would cause unemployment and possibly financial liquidation. What happened before 1972 is that entrepreneurs were convinced that the state would not allow this to happen and therefore investment was maintained and one of the most powerful downward cumulative factors was eliminated.

Since 1972 we have had the first hint of a recurrence of the prewar type of cyclical phenomena: a boom evoked by strong speculation on the stock exchange and property markets, and violent upward movement of the prices of freely traded commodities and, after the turning point, a fall in investment such as we have not experienced since the war.

Under these circumstances government intervention *ipso facto* must appear to be destabilising. Government must at certain points of the upward movement intervene, either because domestic prices threaten to get out of hand or because the balance of payments shows an unacceptable deficit. Rising unemployment is the obverse actuating factor in the case of slumps. Whatever the particular reason or timing in any particular case there can be no doubt that sooner or later the point will come when one or other of these reasons will force positive intervention. But that intervention must be strong enough to break the boom – and *mutatis mutandis*, end the slump – that is to say, destroy foolish speculative expectations (or alter excessive pessimism) which are the unavoidable concomitant of the boom (or the slump) and which cannot be selectively and discriminatingly checked by indirect (that is, fiscal or monetary) means. If, however, the intervention is strong enough to alter the mood then it must from that moment onwards, when the psychological change occurs, appear to be excessive. This follows because some of the strongest of the forces which sustained the boom (such as current expenditure out of capital gains, or investment projects undertaken in the mood of excessive optimism) are suddenly eliminated (and vice versa). With the loss or annihilation of asset values bankruptcies follow (*mutatis mutandis*, asset values are created, and capital gains stimulate demand).

The story of the efforts of successive Chancellors of the Exchequer, Butler, Maudling and Barber, to reverse the recession they themselves had engendered (because the previous expansion had to be checked) are as good examples as the story of the fight of the Federal Reserve from 1928 onwards to halt speculation, which no one would deny was excessive. If any tentative suggestions are at all justified we must accept the fact that the government, in managing the economic system, must appear to be destabilising, because by turning optimism into pessimism (or vice versa) it causes a reverse cumulative movement which cannot be halted by conventional global measures without falling into the opposite evil. This does not mean, however, as a growing number of economists seem to believe, that without government intervention there would have been more stability. The surmise is more plausible – and in these matters one can only surmise – that without government intervention the boom might have further fed on itself and gone wilder with an inevitably sharper crash at the end. It is much more likely that the subsequent decline would have ended in panic liquidation than in a gradual slowing down.

Thus the conclusion which both the monetarists and some Cambridge authors draw – that a fainéant policy of holding the ring through a (small) but steady expansion of government expenditure, or of the money supply, could stabilise activity by monetary or fiscal means alone – is a complete *non sequitur.* It follows that more and more direct controls and positive agreements on incomes (that is, positive intervention) are needed to harmonise full employment and stability. Decontrol, denationalisation, and a return to 'global' and indirect policy measures will perpetuate unemployment for fear of inflation.

It is evident that in many countries a majority of voters might prefer heavy unemployment to inflation, but Keynes's attitude was fairly clearcut. To quote Sir Alec from Keynes himself: 'other more reasonable, less punitive, means (than unemployment) must be found'.[15] But as Sir Alec says he did not claim to have found them: 'the task of keeping efficiency wages reasonably stable (I am sure they will creep up steadily in spite of our best efforts) is a political rather than an economic problem'.[16] I am certain that Keynes, who was basically a great humanitarian, would have striven for a political solution, and such a solution would have implied a great deal of more discriminating, more direct controls based on a social compact, including wages and differentials, prices, taxation and social services, than either side of industry would tolerate. We shall no doubt limp on with some inflation, quite heavy unemployment, and much bitterness, until the lesson has been learnt not only by industry but by economists.

I cannot do better than close my remarks with a quotation from Lord Kahn's Keynes Lecture:[17]

> The question what Keynes would be advocating today is, of course, a nonsense question. Were he alive today – apart from the fact that he would be 91 years old – his own ideas would have developed enormously; under his influence the ideas of others would have developed on different lines; and the economic situation of the country, and of the world, would be different.
>
> Keynes often used to remark to me that he enjoyed the advantage of waking up every morning like a newborn babe, entirely uncommitted to what he had thought or advocated previously.

NOTES

1. Brookings Institution (Washington: 1970), especially Chapters 1 and 2.

2. Lionel Robbins, *An Essay on the Nature and Significance of Economic Science* (London: 1932), p. 107.

3. 'The Economic Consequences of Mr Churchill', p. 17. *Collected Writings*, Vol. IX, p. 218.

4. The most volatile such as 'brokers' loans on account of others', and some short-term assets, as liquid as those included in 'money', were left out.

5. See the sharp attacks on Friedman's paper (with Meiselman) 'The Relative Stability of Monetary Velocity and the Investment Multiplier in the US 1897–1958', in *Stabilisation Policies, Commission on Money and Credit* (Englewood Cliffs, N.J.: 1963).

6. 'Revolution and Counterrevolution in Economics', *Encounter* (1971), p. 23.

7. *Value and Capital* (London: 1938). He has in the meanwhile changed his views. In his *The Crisis of Keynesian Economics* (Oxford: 1974), p. 24, he states boldly: 'A pure flexprice theory, of that type, is not realistic, though it may be instructive. It is doubtless less realistic than a pure fixprice theory. But a pure fixprice theory is itself not wholly realistic. For speculative markets (such as markets for staple commodities, not to speak of financial markets) do exist'.

8. M. Friedman, 'The Role of Monetary Policy', *American Economic Review* (March 1968), p. 8.

9. F. Modigliani, 'The Monetarist Controversy or, Should we Forsake

Stabilisation Policies?' *American Economic Review* (March 1977), Sec. II.C.

10. N. Kaldor, 'A Model of the Trade Cycle', *Economic Journal* (March 1940). An even earlier contribution was R. Frisch, 'Propagation Problems and Impulse Problems in Dynamic Economics', in *Essays in Honour of Gustav Cassel* (London: 1933).

11. *Britain's Economic Prospects*, ed. R. E. Caves (London and Washington: 1968), especially Chapter 1 by R. A. and P. B. Musgrave.

12. Ninth Report from the Expenditure Committee, House of Commons, *Inflation and the Balance of Payments*, especially Sections 48–53. Their monetarist conclusions were not supported by logical argument.

13. (London: 1929), especially Chapters 3, 5, 7 and 12.

14. Kaldor, 'A Model of the Trade Cycle', op. cit.

15. Quoted by Lord Kahn, 'On Re-Reading Keynes'. *Fourth Keynes Lecture in Economics.* Reprint from the *Proceedings of the British Academy*, Vol. LX (Oxford University Press: 1974), p. 21.

16. Ibid., p. 25.

17. Ibid., p. 32.

# Session 2

## INTRODUCTION

*Professor M. Vile* (Chairman)

To open the second session this afternoon it is my pleasure to introduce to you Dr Robert Skidelsky from the Polytechnic of North London. He is a prominent political scientist and historian, particularly of the interwar period, with a biography of Sir Oswald Mosley and a history of the Labour government 1929–31 to his credit. He is now engaged on a new biography of Keynes. Since the United States has always been one of the supposed bastions of free enterprise capitalism, and 1976 marks the 200th anniversary of the Declaration of Independence, this year's seminar could hardly escape from a discussion of the influence of Keynesianism on American economic and political life. Dr Skidelsky, who has recently returned from America, has kindly agreed to address us on the subject of 'The American Response to Keynes'.

## THE AMERICAN RESPONSE TO KEYNES

*Dr R. Skidelsky*

### I

The acceptance of Keynes by America is commonly presented, at least by most economists who have described it, as the triumph of truth over error. The drama takes place on a high intellectual plane. It is between two rival concepts of the budget, the one asserting that the aim of fiscal policy should be to balance the budget, the other seeing it as the instrument for keeping the economy at full employment. Each concept is based on a different economic theory. The one sees the economy as self-restoring in the absence of interference, the other believes that it will remain stuck in depression unless continually pushed by the government. Over a 30-year period the second, or Keynesian, theory has gradually triumphed over the first. The completed process has been described as the Keynes–Kennedy Revolution, a coupling particularly dear to the heart of the American liberal economist. Although the economist likes to present the struggle between the two theories in intellectual terms, he emphaticaly denies that the two positions were of equal intellectual merit. Keynes had sufficiently exposed the intellectual errors of his opponents in his *General Theory*. The persistence of error was to be explained largely in terms of the stupidity of the 'practical men', an explanation much favoured by Keynes himself in accounting for hostility to his proposals. The final triumph of Keynesian ideas must be seen as a 'conversion' of the practical men by President Kennedy's economic advisers in the early 1960s.

The partiality of most economists for a view of the matter only slightly caricatured above must be ascribed to professional bias, not to say self-interest. It emphasises the power of ideas, especially economic ideas, to change the world. It also casts early American converts to Keynesianism in the role of folk heroes struggling against the mighty forces of ignorance and reaction. I must confess to a certain scepticism. For one thing, it has never appeared to me, as an historian, that the 'truth' of an idea has been the major determinant of its success in the competitive, real-world struggle between different ideas, and this applies even to that narrower and more highly structured class of ideas to which the label 'theory' may be applied. Secondly, it seemed to me that the Keynesian successes in America were rather too easily won for the picture of an enlightened *élite* struggling against massive hostility to be entirely plausible. The main penalty for being a Keynesian in the late 1930s was almost instant appointment to a government job – hardly adequate proof of martyrdom.

I detected, in short, a certain discrepancy between the Keynesian claim to be revolutionary and the ease with which a certain type and a certain version of Keynesian ideas were assimilated into mainstream American life. It seemed that those ideas were by no means as unwelcome or unacceptable to the powerholders in American society as the classic Keynesian accounts imply. Against the Keynesian claim to be revolutionary, we must balance the fact that Keynes turns out to have 'saved capitalism'. So we would, at the very least, expect the hostility of men of conservative disposition to new ideas to be tempered by a certain shrewd appreciation of self-interest.

Before considering what, in my view, the function of Keynesian ideas in American politics has been, I want to recall in more detail the usual version of Keynes's coming to America.

## II

The conventional account of the American response to Keynes opens with the publication of his *General Theory* in 1936, and the start of the conversion of the economics profession. It is now generally agreed that the New Deal before this point had been innocent of Keynesian ideas. True, there were some proto-Keynesians in Washington–Marriner Eccles at the Federal Reserve Board who ascribed his radicalism to the fact that he had never been to university and therefore had no economics to unlearn; his research director Lauchlin Currie, and General Hugh 'Ironpants' Johnson, head of the National Recovery Administration. But their spending ideas had little influence with Roosevelt who repeatedly said that he wanted to reduce public spending and balance the budget. The severity of the crisis, and the need to do something, rather than a new theory, put this goal perpetually beyond reach.

Nor had Keynes's own visits to America had much effect. He came to Chicago in 1931, saying that 'there is nothing President Hoover can do that an earthquake could not do better'. He saw Roosevelt in June 1934, leaving him quite baffled. He gave Roosevelt's Secretary of Labour, Miss Frances Perkins, a simple exposition of the multiplier in terms of grocery purchases, which he regarded with considerable wonder.[1] On the same trip, he was visited in his hotel room in Washington by the agricultural economist, Calvin Hoover. Using Keynes's bathroom to wash in, Hoover was careful to take a clean towel from the pile without disturbing the others. Entering the bathroom after him, Keynes swept the whole pile to the floor in lordly fashion, explaining, as he crumpled them up, that his method of using towels would do more to stimulate employment than Hoover's. These interventions had, not surprisingly, little effect on American economic policy.

But with the publication of the *General Theory* all this changed. The effect at Harvard was particularly profound among economists of tender years. 'Bliss was it in that dawn to be alive, but to be young was very heaven', recalled Paul Samuelson many years later.[2] It was a general experience, moving many young economists to poetic expression. As Galbraith put it: 'The old economics was still taught by day. But in the evening and almost every evening from 1936 onwards almost everyone in the Harvard community discussed Keynes'.[3] From this conversion process emerged a Keynesian *school* 'not in that loose sense in which some historians of economics speak of a French, German, Italian school, but a genuine one which is a sociological entity, namely, a group that professes allegiance to One Master and One Doctrine, and has its inner circle, its propagandists, its watchwords, its esoteric and its popular doctrine'.[4]

According to the conventional view, the main reason for this development is simple. The *General Theory* filled the need for an explanation, in terms of fundamental economic theory, of why unemployment occurred. It was the lack of such an explanation before 1936 that perpetuated the hegemony of the orthodox economics and damned as unsound practical proposals for government spending, including Keynes's own. True, there were a number of *political* and *institutional* explanations for unemployment, and also fragments of theoretical explanation in the works of 'heretics' like Hobson and the underconsumptionists. But these latter had been quite unable to upset the reigning orthodoxy; indeed, their work was regarded as intellectually inferior. Keynes provided a theory of unemployment which filled this gap. The fact that it was empirically quite untested, as Professor Corry has pointed out, was less important than that it was at once elegant, logical, operational. He consolidated previous discussions of the causes of economic fluctuations into relationships among a small number of variables. In particular, he showed how employment depended on the level of aggregate output, and how that level could remain too low to provide full employment – something which the classics had denied. In such a situation, government spending was needed to restore full employment.

The next phase of the story concerns the creation of a Keynesian wedge in the economics profession. Alvin Hansen plays a prominent part. He came to Harvard from Minnesota in 1937, an older man but a recent convert, a lucid and indefatigable evangelist for Keynesian ideas and, in his stagnation theory, the author of 'the only truly original American extension of Keynesian economics until at least the 1950s'.[5] His seminar on fiscal policy at Harvard 'was a major focus of both theoretical and practical discussion'.[6] Alvin Hansen, Seymour Harris, and Paul Samuelson were the three academics who diffused Keynesian theory through the economics profession. By 1940, as a result of their proselytising, Keynes 'had acquired a greater number of fervent disciples [in America] than in his own country'.[7]

This conventional account of Keynes's early appeal to young economists leaves out at least two striking ingredients in that appeal. The first was its political radicalism. The *General Theory*, as Schumpeter has brilliantly observed, was 'the final result of a long struggle to make [Keynes's] vision of our age analytically operative'.[8] It was Keynes's social vision, quite as much as the theory into which he translated it, that proved so attractive to the young economists; or rather that vision as elaborated by Alvin Hansen. Hansen argued that there existed an inexorable tendency for private investment to fall short of full-employment saving in a mature economy. Keeping full employment would require not only a substantial redistribution of income (to increase consumption relative to saving) but also a permanently higher level of government spending. This version of Keynesianism was perfectly calculated to appeal to political radicals. Without being a socialist himself, Hansen linked Keynesian theory to socialism. The economic manifesto by seven Harvard and Tufts economists, published in October 1938, proposed a 'vigorous expansion of the public sector of the economy, sharp increases in the progression of the tax system, indefinite increases in the public debt, enlargement of old-age benefits, assistance programmes for health and education, and massive commitments to housing and urban development'.[9] One of the signatories, Paul Sweezy, later became the most famous American Marxist economist. Keynesianism, much against Keynes's wishes, thus entered American life as a left-wing political tendency. This enhanced its appeal to radical economists, but obviously enormously complicated the problem of its winning acceptance from the business community.

Hansen's stagnation theory also appealed to young ambitious policy-makers by providing a rationale for the permanent direction of economic life by an *élite* of economists. Under *laissez-faire*, there was no government role for economists, because there was no economic role for the government. In the Depression, economic policy of the modern kind had started up, but it was in the hands of amateurs and cranks. In the Keynesian political economy, public policy would be handed over to the professional economists, who alone would understand what needed to be done. We should neither overestimate nor underestimate the force of academic empire-building in winning acceptance for new social theories. In the nineteenth century, it was, on the whole, historians who pronounced on grave issues of public policy. With the rise of social engineering, economists and sociologists have taken their place. As an historian, I view this change with a certain regret.

Hansen's promises were speedily fulfilled. The next stage in America's assimilation of Keynes was the translation, almost *en masse*, of the Keynesian segment of the economics profession into the Washington bureaucracy. Both by his own, and others', accounts, Lauchlin Currie, moving from the Federal Reserve Board to the White House in 1939 as Roosevelt's main economic adviser, was the leading Washington recruiter of Keynesians. Whenever anyone in the Administration wanted an economist, Currie rang up Hansen who supplied him with one. There was a veritable emigration from Harvard to Washington which must have left Hansen's famous seminar somewhat denuded. Hansen himself, and Galbraith, arrived in 1940. 'By the end of the thirties, writes Galbraith, 'Currie had established an informal network of converts extending into all the fiscally significant agencies. All remained in close communication on ideas and policies. Neither Currie nor any of those involved regarded this as conspiracy. It merely seemed the necessary and sensible thing to do'.[10]

Here again, a footnote is necessary. After the war, both Whittaker Chambers and Elizabeth Bentley alleged that Currie's recruiting policies (and those of Harry Dexter White at the Treasury) were based less on the search for Keynesian expertise than the promotion of Communist sympathies within key government departments. Despite an extensive literature this allegation has been neither convincingly established nor disproved.[11] Keynesian and Communist affiliations were not mutually exclusive in the 1930s and early 1940s, when domestic reform, antifascism, and support for the Soviet Union seemed to go harmoniously together. The point to note is that it was the political radicalism of the early Keynesians, rather than the doctrine itself, which affected the wider American response to the Keynesian Revolution.

At this stage, the 'real world' is generally conceded to have given Keynesian ideas a helping hand. The war, and preparations for it, are agreed to have speeded, though not caused, the translation of Keynesian theory into economic policy. War gave an opportunity to test Keynesian theory in two major ways. First, it provided the setting for the first systematic attempt to spend one's way to full employment. Currie seems to have played a key part in converting Roosevelt to this with his memorandum of 18 March 1940 in which he argued that only full-employment output could provide America with both guns *and* butter, in other words, prepare her for war without sacrificing social goals.[12] Walter Salant worked out the size of the deficits needed to achieve full employment. Secondly, once full employment had been achieved, Keynesian theory suggested the fiscal policy required to eliminate the 'inflationary gap'; that is, to ensure a non-inflationary allocation of resources between civilian consumption and military spending.

The success of both undertakings depended on quantitative measurements of the Keynesian aggregates which had been worked out by Simon Kuznets; their implementation brought a new flood of Keynesians into the government, especially into the Treasury and special wartime agencies. It was the success of the wartime full-employment experiment that supposedly convinced a wider public that it was both feasible and desirable for the government to maintain a high peacetime level of employment; hence the passing of the Employment Act of 1946. Summing up the Keynesian experience to that date, Professor Jones has written '. . . some 20 to 50 economists had created a revolution in American policy'.[13] They had done so by showing that Keynesian theory worked, in other words, it did what it claimed it would.

At this point in the conventional account, the 'practical' men step in to prevent the full flowering of the American Keynesian Revolution. Business opposition forced the dropping of the radical aspects of the Employment Act of 1946; and was able to confine postwar economic policy to an impoverished form of Keynesianism based on 'built-in stabilisers'. It had long been recognised that public revenues rose and fell automatically with the economy, whereas public spending remained the same unless deliberately changed. If both tax rates and spending were held constant, the budget would move into automatic deficit in a recession and automatic surplus in a boom. The first would mitigate the recession, the second flatten out the boom, all without any human interference. It was a frustrating time for the dedicated Keynesians. After their heady wartime experience, the Eisenhower years in particular were a bitter disappointment. Businessmen still clung to their archaic notions of a balanced budget and their fanatical resistance to 'state' interference. Ike was absurdly worried about inflation. Meanwhile, the economy was being run below its full potential. Not enough new jobs were being created to match growing population and increasing productivity, thus causing unemployment to drift steadily upwards through the 1950s and early 1960s. Built-in stabilisers kept the new generation of macroeconomists, by now distinctly middle-aged, out of their rightful inheritance.

But salvation was at hand in the person of President Kennedy. The story of the 1964 tax-cut, as told by Arthur Okun, James Tobin and others, has become legendary among all consenting economists. It was the Harvard of the 1930s writ large. The America of the early 1960s, we are led to believe, was engaged in passionate discussion of fiscal drag. This was not an exotic form of attire, but the idea that in the absence of tax-cuts or spending increases the growth of the economy makes the budget increasingly deflationary through gradually increasing tax revenue. Soon the President's Council of Economic Advisers put forward an even more radical idea for public consumption. The goal of the balanced budget, they said, should be finally, and ruthlessly, expunged from public policy, in the interests of logical consistency. The budget should be planned to yield a full employment surplus or deficit such that full-employment saving and private investment would balance at the 'natural' growth rate. As Professor Tobin put it: 'Depending on economic circumstances . . . the principle may suggest either a surplus or a deficit; only by accident would it suggest exact balance'.[14]

The revolutionary principle in President Kennedy's tax bill of 1963 was that taxes should be cut when the economy was already well on the way to recovery from the recession of 1961–62. This signified final rejection of the idea that 'natural forces' could be relied upon to push the economy back to full employment. In future, the government would commit itself not just to preventing slumps, but ensuring that the economy lived up to its full-employment and growth potential. Greater intellectual understanding was the key to the political success of this new departure. Only in the 1960s, according to Professor Tobin, did the 'view of the economic mechanism commonly accepted by men of affairs' finally move into line with the 'models' that economists had long worked with; only then were the 'phobias about public spending, budget deficits, and internal public debt . . . largely overcome or forgotten'.[15] Amidst the euphoria of this intellectual triumph, it was left to Herbert Stein to make the telling point that '. . the tax-cut of 1964, commonly viewed as the final defeat of budget-balancing, was also the great victory of conservative fiscal policy'.[16]

## III

It would be wrong to regard the economists' account as a travesty of why Keynesian ideas triumphed. They did conquer most of the economics profession, partly at least for logical reasons; and in practice they worked, especially in wartime. But to leave it there would be highly misleading. What the economists' version on the whole ignores is that the reasons which make a theory acceptable to a profession are very different from those which recommend it to practical men.[17] Even for economists the appeal of Keynesian theory was reinforced by other factors. This was so to a much greater degree outside the profession. Practical men are interested not in the truth of a theory but in its usefulness. (Maurice Cowling reminds us that 'politicians understand as much as they need to of the situations in which they work. This need not be much.'[18]). The main use of a theory is to legitimise (and no doubt make more efficient) a course of action desirable for other reasons. We may say that a certain version of Keynesian economic policy gained ground in America because it was the most generally politically acceptable of the various panaceas which emerged from the Depression era.

In order to develop this point, we will need to clarify the nature of the opposition to Keynesian ideas. It is often claimed that the American tradition, being one of dogmatic private enterprise and rugged individualism, is violently hostile to all forms of government interference. America, it is argued, has been built up of people who sought to escape from governments; hence the hold of the 'negative concept of liberty'. All this is very true. But it must be qualified in two ways. First, the extreme *laissez-faire* phase was confined to the middle 50 years of the nineteenth century. Both before and after, *laissez-faire* was heavily criticised. Since the 1880s, *laissez-faire* has been in almost continuous retreat. Indeed, from today's perspective, it is the extreme libertarian interlude of the 1920s which appears paradoxical, not the managed economy of the New Deal and after. Secondly, side by side with individualism, there has always been a very strong strain of activism. There is no American counterpart to the European fatalism which accepts bad times as a visitation from God, to be endured, rather than cured. Americans have always been problem-solvers, favouring especially quantitative solutions involving power and numbers. The American, writes Henry Steel Commager, was 'accustomed to prosperity, resented anything that interfered with it, and regarded any prolonged lapse from it as an outrage against nature'.[19] Activism and individualism could be combined, as in Herbert Spencer's social dynamics; but after the 1880s, with the 'closing of the frontier', problem-solving was increasingly seen in terms of collective action. This was the premise of Progressivism.

A more narrow claim is that American businessmen were uniquely opposed to state intervention as much, on the grounds that it was incompatible with 'free enterprise' and 'capitalism'.[20] Certainly, American business rhetoric was more strident and abstract on this point than that of its European counterpart.[21] But rhetoric in his case is not an adequate guide to reality. The clamour of special interests for government intervention on their behalf was not noticeably less in America than Europe. On the other hand, the doctrine of high wages was much *more* highly developed in America, and this was helpful to Keynesian ideas. We may note, too, the native American multiplier tradition in the writings of Foster and Catchings, and in the folklore of railway development.

Business ways of thinking about economic life were thus not nearly as hostile to the Keynesian approach as has commonly been supposed. But, of course, the ideas had to be properly packaged for American consumption; and they had to win their way in competition with rival panaceas for economic distress, in which America was particularly luxuriant. Careful analysis of business opposition to the New Deal shows that it was invariably opposition to specific measures, rather than to budget deficits as such. Once intervention could take different forms, business opposition would die away, even though some of the rhetoric would remain. Even in the 1930s, the main opposition to Roosevelt came from small businessmen, represented by the National Union of Manufacturers, rather than big business, whose representatives, sitting on the Business Advisory Council, endorsed most of the New Deal measures.[22]

Keynes himself never accepted the inevitability of business opposition to his plans. He insisted time and again that he had come to save capitalism, not destroy it. His explanation of business hostility to the New Deal is first conveyed in an open letter to Roosevelt published in the *New York Times* on 31 December 1933. In it Keynes made a vital distinction between 'reform' and 'recovery', urging priority for the latter, and arguing that the National Recovery Administration was in fact impeding recovery by damaging business confidence. He was to pursue this line throughout the 1930s. For example, on 25

March 1938 he wrote to Roosevelt: 'You must either give more encouragement to business or take over more of their functions yourself... Your present policies seem to presume that you possess more power than you actually have'.[23]

What Keynes, of course, wanted, was a recovery programme based on government loan expenditure.[24] This could take a variety of forms – subsidies to business and agriculture, spending on relief, public works, and so on. There would have been little initial opposition to such a policy. Pressure for a big spending programme had been building up in Congress all through Hoover's presidency. Many economists were in favour.[25] Senator Wagner wanted $12 billion to be spent in one year – an enormous sum. The big spenders in the Administration wanted $4 billion to $5 billion. Roosevelt spurned them. His biggest spending programmes before 1938 were imposed on him by Congress, and the veterans' bonus of 1936 over his veto. Once Depression struck, the American political system revealed a built-in bias towards increased Federal spending, stemming from the closeness of the relationship between Congress and particular interests; more so than the British system where an aloof mandarin class governed ostentatiously in the 'national interest'.

There was an even sturdier native tradition of inflation. Inflation has always had an appeal to a debtor country. The American entrepreneurial tradition was rooted in land speculation. The country was built on debt and has lived off it ever since. With a business structure and psychology geared to debt, monetary manipulation was more popular in America than in England. The United States was the home of both popular and academic monetarism. Only the first, that of the Greenbackers and Free Silverites, was inflationist; but it was the academic tradition, represented by Irving Fisher, that provided intellectual support for Roosevelt's bizarre attempts to raise the price level in 1933 by buying gold: 'the gold standard on the booze', as Keynes described it.

However, the point is that the New Deal did not proceed very far in these directions. Spending was undertaken reluctantly, and in small amounts. The monetary experiments were soon abandoned, possibly too soon. To the New Dealers, these were mere palliatives. To them recovery meant reform. Deficits and monetary manipulation were short-term temporary measures, pending the adoption of basic structural reforms. These were no part of Keynes's theory, or policy proposals. But they were what frightened businessmen.

This New Deal confusion between 'recovery' and 'reform' is not hard for a European to grasp. It is part of the perpetual dilemma of social democracy. At this period, it consisted in applying an older critique of capitalism, worked out in the nineteenth and early twentieth centuries, to the problems of the Depression. It was not that the older critique was wrong. No doubt there were non-Keynesian routes out of the Depression; even towards Utopia. The trouble was that the power shifts necessary to apply these remedies had not taken place – not in Europe, even less so in the United States. Power remained in the hands of the business classes. They could no longer, unaided, make the economic mechanism work. But their lack of confidence in political arrangements could keep it from working. And no political force existed capable of dispossessing them. In such a situation, policies based on the premise of destroying or superseding or hating capitalism were doomed to frustration.

Roosevelt understood this. Like Keynes, he proclaimed himself 'the best friend the profit system ever had'.[26] The N.R.A. had something in it for all the main interest-groups: business, labour, agriculture; it was an essay in 'interest-group democracy'; the government saw itself as the 'broker state'; for its rhetoric (and some of its practice) it drew heavily on wartime precedents. This was akin to the slow realisation in Europe that if government interventions were to have good results, they must have capitalist support. Indeed, this realisation came quicker in the United States, where there was no vigorous native socialist tradition, than in Europe. The problem was to find a formula and policy adequate to the recovery consensus that Roosevelt was trying to create. He never found the answer in the 1930s; he stumbled on it during the war, and died without ever understanding what it was.

Roosevelt's first 100 days revived business confidence, as is shown by the remarkable recovery of production which took place, without fiscal stimulus, during the second quarter of 1933.[27] It was less the specific measures taken in his first period than the unsettling ideas of his entourage that was responsible for the growth of business opposition after March 1934.

The social vision of the New Deal, which drew intellectuals into government service under Roosevelt, and must be sharply distinguished from the emergency spending measures, was rooted in the Progressivist critique of concentrated economic power. For the older Progressives it had been the concentration that was evil; for the newer ones, it was its uncontrolled character. In policy, the difference was between breaking up big business or subjecting it to national planning. The older tradition of Brandeis and Frankfurter, represented in the Administration by men like Arnold, Cohen, and Corcoran, was that of the trust-busters who wanted to relieve the Depression by 'atomising' business and restoring the market. But the updated version was more significant at the beginning. Both Tugwell and Berle, two members of Roosevelt's first Brains Trust, saw uncontrolled economic power as responsible for the Depression. First, it made the system much more liable to severe distress by delaying necessary adjustments to new conditions: Galbraith's much later account of the Wall Street collapse of 1929, centring on the destabilising role of the investment trusts, is in this tradition.[28] Secondly, the accumulation of undistributed corporate surplus (savings) prevented a rise in consumer spending – a Hobsonian explanation – leading to overproduction and mass unemployment. This analysis was not much different from that of the older Progressives. The newer ones accepted, however, that size had come to stay. The remedy was to subject it to the disciplines of public planning and income redistribution. The codes of the N.R.A. were designed both to establish a government–business planning partnership and to raise workers' income through statutory support for collective bargaining. But Tugwell and the planners wanted to go much further. Tugwell, who held high office in the first New Deal, envisaged a planning board for each industry. On top of this would come a central planning board staffed by disinterested experts, allocating capital investment and controlling prices.[29] It was because some early New Deal measures seemed to portent later developments along these lines that conservative opinion became alarmed. And it was precisely this centralised planning approach that Keynes urged Roosevelt to drop.

Some of the institutional arguments were well-founded, and measures to upgrade the position of American Labour and reform the Banks and Stock Exchange permanently improved the working of the American economy. But certain economic policies deriving from the institutionalist perspective hindered recovery and thus complicated Roosevelt's political position. First, the emphasis on 'overproduction' led to policies designed to restrict output to the existing level of demand, which were deflationary in their effect. Secondly, the preoccupation with putting farmers, workers, and industrialists into a 'balanced' relationship with each other ignored the problem of insufficiency of overall demand. Thus Tugwell's view that enlarging farm income relative to city income would increase demand for industrial goods ignored the fact that such a policy would diminish urban demand by as much.[30]

In the period of the first New Deal, business felt threatened by the spectre of state control. The prospect held out by the second New Deal was that of punitive taxation. The failure of half-hearted collectivism to produce either recovery or consensus had forced a change of direction in 1935. The subsequent debate over whether Roosevelt moved to the Left to undercut the appeal of Huey Long, Coughlin, Townsend and the redistributors, or to the Right in response to business and legal opposition to the N.R.A., is a tribute to his ambiguous legacy. In fact, he did both, and also responded to the actual problems of the economy. The collectivists were dropped. But at the same time, Roosevelt did respond to a new radical mood in Congress and the country. This popular radicalism was quite different from the austere planning approach of the mandarins; it gave the second New Deal, in Richard Hofstadter's words, a 'social democratic tinge'. Its most important legislative fruit was the Revenue Act of 1935, by which Roosevelt increased rates on earned and inherited income and on undistributed corporate profits.

In retrospect, the Revenue Act can be seen as the centrepiece of a new economic and political strategy. It reflects Roosevelt's more determined quest for a balanced budget. It was designed to please Labour by 'soaking the rich' and punishing them for their sabotage of the N.R.A. Finally, it was designed to alleviate the Depression by redistributing wealth (the under-consumptionist argument).

The furious business opposition to the Act – it created, according to Leuchtenberg 'deeper business resentment than any other New Deal measure'[31] – exposes the hollowness of business demands for fiscal virtue. For the Revenue Act was undoubtedly a step in the direction of fiscal orthodoxy as it was then understood. But unbalanced budgets were never the real issue. The opposition to big spending arose not because it portended an unbalanced budget, but because it did not – in other words, it portended higher taxes to balance it. Low spending, in other words, was the best guarantee of low taxes, the primary business interest. Paradoxically, Roosevelt's claims to fiscal orthodoxy alarmed the businessmen far more than their absence would have done.

Whether the 1937–38 recession was caused by the blow to business confidence brought about by the shift to the Left, or the reduction in the budget deficit brought about by new taxation, is unclear. What is clear is that the recession marked the failure of Roosevelt's second attempt to devise an agreed recovery programme. Politically, the New Deal was trapped in a hopeless dilemma: the reforms designed to help the poor who made up the bulk of the President's following antagonised business on which wealth production depended. The result was a great deal of reform, but incomplete recovery, despite bouts of deficit spending. (The dilemma has been familiar in Britain in most periods of Labour Government.) It was in this situation that Keynesian policy started to acquire its residual role of doing whatever all other means in combination had failed to do.

This is evident from Professor Stein's review of the options facing Roosevelt at the end of 1937. He could press on firmly with Morgenthau's policy of economy and a balanced budget. He could remove the anti-business aspects of the New Deal, mainly the undistributed profits tax, and thereby hope to revive private investment. He might restore the planning features of N.R.A., in so far as this could be done voluntarily, in an effort to sustain wages and investment. He might attack concentrated economic power on Corcoran's hypothesis that the monopolists had 'simply priced themselves out of the market, and priced themselves into a slump'.[32] Or he might try to spend his way out of the Depression.

Of these alternatives, the last was coming to be seen as the most attractive, both politically and intellectually. The balanced budget had no important political force behind it (one wonders whether it ever did). The business demand for an end to progressive taxation as the price for lifting the 'strike of capital' was more serious, but could not be met without destroying Roosevelt's political base. (One proposal of future significance was Beardsley Ruml's to cancel the instalment of income tax payments due in December 1937). Institutional reform seemed too slow, and, besides, faced the prospect of further Supreme Court vetoes. On the other hand, there were now important vested Administration interests in public spending; the machinery existed for quick implementation; and spending programmes had built up a politically important clientele in Congress, the party, state and local governments, and among their direct beneficiaries. Intellectually, with the publication of the *General Theory*, spending policy had acquired much greater intellectual prestige; and young Keynesians were starting to come to Washington. In a memorandum of 8 November 1937, Lauchlin Currie, Leon Henderson and Isador Lubin argued persuasively that purchasing power had fallen off due to the cut in the government deficit. On 14 April 1938, Roosevelt took the plunge, sending Congress his plan for 'spending' America out of Depression. His New Deal had started with the idea of the Corporate State, moved towards a Welfare State in its second phase, and ended up producing a Keynesian State, with corporate and welfare trimmings.[33]

It is important not to exaggerate this 'fiscal revolution'. Roosevelt only asked for \$1·5 billion of 'extra' money – money beyond what was needed to pay for existing programmes. The recovery was far from spectacular: in August 1939, economic activity was still below its mid-1937 peak. Moreover, Keynesian policy had still not emerged in a politically acceptable, and therefore usable, form.

There were two reasons for this. In the Administration, 'recovery' was still bound up with 'reform'. As we have seen, the earliest Keynesians were radical not only in economic theory, but also in social policy. They wanted to pursue the collectivist and social democratic goals of the earlier New Deals by means of fiscal policy. This meant more spending, and spending in the public sector, rather than tax-cutting. The second reason was institutional. The small size of the budget in relation to GNP meant that to achieve a substantial fiscal effect one would need to increase spending rather than cut taxes. But large government spending programmes were politically suspect; they were slow in effect and gave rise to bureaucratic empires vulnerable to charges of corruption, incompetence, and tyranny. As long as Keynesian policy, for political and institutional reasons, was identified exclusively with government spending, it was bound to seem a threat to both private business and individual freedom, uniting businessmen and libertarians against it. The President's so-called Spend–Lend Bill of 1939 was rejected by Congress. The fiscal route to recovery was temporarily barred. The New Deal 'never demonstrated that it could achieve prosperity in peacetime'.[34]

The Second World War not merely gave Keynesian economics a helpful hand; it was crucial to its political success, and thus to the political success of the New Deal. I do not thereby wish to imply that Roosevelt and the Administration Keynesians sought war in order to liberate fiscal policy from domestic constraints. But there is much evidence to suggest that Roosevelt's advisers saw rearmament as the only way of generating Congressional support for massive spending; and by 1940 Roosevelt badly needed a successful employment programme for his re-election. In combination, these two considerations did suggest playing up the dangers to American security. All foreign policy involves an interplay between domestic and international politics; and Roosevelt's response to German and Japanese expansionism was no exception.

The favourable change in conditions brought about by the Second World War has three aspects. First, war and war preparations created a large enough budget to enable tax variations, deliberate or automatic, to replace spending decisions as the central tool of Keynesian policy. The war had greatly expanded the size of the budget on both its spending and revenue sides, as the radical Keynesians had demanded. But this very fact made tax-cutting a more plausible anti-Depression remedy than spending increases. With the introduction of PAYE, tax-cuts could take immediate effect; they required no elaborate administrative machinery; and with the spread of tax-paying to the majority, they would please a large constituency.

Secondly, the war discredited radical Keynesianism by destroying its central hypothesis, the stagnation theory. War was like that earthquake which Keynes had recommended as the solution to Hoover's problems. Convinced that 'natural forces' would never 'take up the slack', the radical Keynesians had argued that government spending be maintained at its wartime levels. In fact, American military spending fell from $95 billion to $15 billion in the year after the war. Instead of the predicted depression, there was a boom. In replacing destroyed productive capacity, in responding to the 'baby boom', in satisfying pent-up consumer demand, 'natural forces' received a stimulus that Hansen claimed had vanished from a 'mature' economy. Additionally, the Anglo-American victory had reopened the frontier: capitalism was no longer confined within national boundaries as had been the case in the 1930s. American hegemony lessened the need for energetic 'national' Keynesianism, both in America and Europe. (In parenthesis, it is worth noting that Keynes's plans for the postwar world order won acceptance only to the extent that they fitted the needs of American power. The United States did take responsibility for 'underwriting' the world economy, but by means of conditional loans, not by provision of automatic overdraft facilities to debtors as the Keynes Plan of 1942 had envisaged.)

Finally, the actual achievement of full employment during the war showed that full-employment policy could become the basis of that elusive consensus sought by Roosevelt in the 1930s. 'Neutral with respect to more divisive goals' it could become 'the flag around which everyone could rally'.[35] The disputes between the planners and trust-busters, Capital and Labour, could be relegated to the background. Keynesian policy came to be appreciated as a method of achieving several desirable political goals simultaneously by means of a single instrument. It did not suffer from the disadvantages of earlier New Deal policies which relied on helping different groups in different ways which contradicted each other, thus aborting overall policy and setting the groups at loggerheads.

Out of these wartime developments, it was possible to fashion a version of Keynesianism which would finally meet the needs of the American situation. The business community's conversion to the goal of full employment was signified by the establishment, by a group of prominent businessmen, of a Committee for Economic Development in 1942. Its chairman was Beardsley Ruml. Ruml was, in Professor Stein's words, 'the main bridge between the thinking of economists on fiscal policy and the thinking of businessmen'.[36] Ruml did more than any other single person to make taxation policy the centrepiece of orthodox American Keynesianism. Tax rates would be set to balance the budget at high employment. This would allow the full influence of the built-in stabilisers, as well as preserving a *pro forma* commitment to budget balancing. Any 'fine tuning' required could be done by monetary policy, although conservative Keynesians tended to mistrust discretionary policy, or policy relying on short-term forecasting.[37] For serious recessions, massive tax-cuts were to be the remedy. Having enjoyed, in war, the benefits of high output and profits, businessmen were determined not to fall back into recession. In the tax-cut they now found they had the ideal instrument for avoiding it. The 'new economics' as it was known could, after all, be married to one of the constants of business thinking – getting taxes down – while simultaneously winning the support of labour. In the Truman and Eisenhower years, Congress and business became enthusiastic fiscal heretics, while the Presidency emerged as the guardian of traditional fiscal orthodoxy. That this was also the underlying, though misunderstood, reality of the 1930s is the most challenging theme of Professor Stein's book.

This perspective suggests an alternative interpretation of the famous tax-cut of 1964. Far from having to educate businessmen in the intricacies of the new economics, as Professor Tobin suggests, President Kennedy and his Keynesian advisers responded to business clamour for a massive tax reduction as economic recovery levelled off in 1962. In so doing, they had to jettison most of the spending programme with which they had earlier hoped to meet the recession.[38] Thus the Keynes–Kennedy Revolution marked not the belated acceptance by Republicans of Keynesian economics, but the final capitulation of Keynesian theory to the needs of American business.

## IV

What I have tried to show is how a revolutionary intellectual breakthrough was converted into a conservative ideology, and in the process to throw some light on the question of why ideas are taken up by society. My account rests on what I hope is a sufficiently sharp distinction between the conversion to, and the use of, ideas. The economics profession was genuinely converted to a radical economic theory and prided itself on its success in converting the practical men. The practical men, however, found the theory useful in preserving the existing economic and social order; hence their willingness to be converted. This, in brief, was the double impact of Keynes on America.

## NOTES

1. Frances Perkins, *The Roosevelt I Knew* (1947), p. 183.
2. H. Stein, *The Fiscal Revolution in America* (1969), p. 163.
3. J. K. Galbraith, *Economics, Peace and Laughter* (1971), p. 48.
4. J. A. Schumpeter, 'John Maynard Keynes 1883–1946', *American Economic Review* (September 1946); reprinted in J. A. Schumpeter, *Ten Great Economists* (1952), pp. 287–8.
5. R. Lekachman, *The Age of Keynes* (1969 edition), p. 111.
6. J. K. Galbraith, *Money, Whence It Came, Where It Went* (1975), p. 228.
7. D. Winch, *Economics and Policy* (1965), p. 220.
8. Schumpeter, op. cit., p. 268.
9. Lekachman, op. cit., p. 132.
10. Galbraith, *Money*, pp. 229–30.
11. For careful surveys, see Herbert Pacher, *Ex-Communist Witnesses* (1962); David Rees, *Harry Dexter White* (1973), pp. 200, 214–18.
12. Byrd L. Jones, 'The Role of Keynesians in Wartime Policy and Postwar Planning 1940–46', Selected Papers from American Economic Association Meeting 27–29 (December 1971), p. 125.
13. Ibid., p. 131. Jones writes that Keynesians 'gained influence because the analytic tools devised by Keynes, Hansen, Currie, Gilbert and a score of others helped them correctly forecast the direction and magnitude of changes in national income'.
14. James Tobin, 'The Intellectual Revolution in US Economic Policy Making', *University of Essex Noel Buxton Lecture* (1966), p. 19.
15. Ibid., p. 1.
16. Stein, op. cit., p. 90.
17. The great exception is Professor Herbert Stein. Those who know his book will realise how much I have relied upon it in this essay.
18. Maurice Cowling, *The Impact of Hitler: British Politics and British Policy 1933–1940* (1975), p. ix.
19. Henry Steele Commager, *The American Mind* (1950), p. 7.
20. This is the thesis of A. E. Holmans, *United States Fiscal Policy 1945–1959* (1961), pp. xi, also Chapter 2. Holmans's argument that it was deficit spending which alarmed businessmen more than anything else about the New Deal (p. 20) is not supported by Stein or Leuchtenberg.
21. Professor Anthony King writes: 'Anyone comparing the rhetoric of American interest groups with that of groups in other countries is bound to be struck by what seems to be the American groups' much greater disposition to state their positions in abstract terms and, in particular, to raise, continually, large questions about the role of the State', *British*

*Journal of Political Science*, 3, p.415.

22. Stein, op. cit., p. 81.

23. Ibid., pp. 108–9.

24. See his draft for a paper he read to the American Political Economy Club, Washington 6 June 1934, in his *Collected Writings*, Vol. xiii, pp. 457–8.

25. Jacob Viner says that Keynes's view that governments should spend more and tax less was commonplace to him and his Chicago colleagues in 1931. *Keynes's General Theory After Three Decades*, ed. R. Lekachman, (1964), p. 263.

26. Q. R. Polenberg (ed.) *Radicalism and Reform in the New Deal* (1972), pp. 4–5.

27. Keynes noted of business activity between March and July 1933 '. . . it is clear that there has been an enormous expansion. This, however, had no sound basis except in business optimism. During that period the administration had done nothing but make a little progress towards liquefying the bank situation'. *Collected Writings*, Vol. xiii, p. 466.

28. J. K. Galbraith, *The Great Crash* (1955).

29. Bernard Sternscher, *Rexford Tugwell and the New Deal* (1964), p. 95f.

30. For a particulary blunt statement of this fallacy, see Rexford G. Tugwell, *F.D.R.: Architect of an Era* (1967), Chapter 14.

31. William E. Leuchtenberg, *Franklin D. Roosevelt and the New Deal 1932–40* (1963), p. 152.

32. Ibid., p. 247.

33. Stein, op. cit., Chapter 6.

34. Leuchtenberg, op. cit., p. 346.

35. Stein, op. cit., p. 172.

36. Ibid., p. 186.

37. I have not had space to go into what Professor Milton Friedman calls the 'rediscovery of money' which also heavily influenced the eventual American version of Keynesianism.

38. Stein, op. cit., pp. 378, 395.

## INTRODUCTION

*Professor M. Vile* (Chairman)

To conclude the formal proceedings of today's seminar Professor Maurice Cranston is going to speak to us on the influence of Keynes on political thought. There is no one more qualified to do this. He is a distinguished political scientist holding the Chair of Political Science at the London School of Economics. He is the authoritative biographer of John Locke and has written and edited books on *Freedom*, *Jean Paul Sartre*, and *Western Political Philosophers*, as well as translating Rousseau's *The Social Contract.* Professor Cranston will bring his wisdom to bear in a paper entitled 'Keynes: His Political Ideas and their Influence'.

# KEYNES: HIS POLITICAL IDEAS AND THEIR INFLUENCE

*Professor M. Cranston*

In many ways Keynes was like Locke. Perhaps he was not quite so important as an economist as Locke was important as a philosopher; but he had the same wide range of interests and the same power of innovative thinking. He was also, like Locke, a liberal; a liberal intellectual who intervened in politics by the same two methods that Locke used – pamphleteering and occasional administrative activity of a high-level and mainly advisory kind. Neither ventured far into politics proper; but both sought to bring about a fusion of the theoretical and the practical forms of reasoning, and both exercised an enormous influence in the backrooms of Westminster by what they said, and throughout the world by what they published. But there is at least one great difference between Locke and Keynes. Locke wrote a systematic treatise of political theory as well as his various political pamphlets, and Locke's liberalism, albeit the subject of some controversy among scholars, has on the whole been fairly well understood. This is not so in the case of Keynes. His liberal political ideas are set forth in different places, scattered throughout his writings. He wrote no single work of political theory as such. Partly because of this, his liberalism has not always been well understood, and has indeed been cruelly misrepresented. No twentieth-century economist has enjoyed more renown than Keynes, and none has been the target of such aggressive criticism.

The two main charges that are brought against Keynes are these: first, that he vitiated the theoretical purity of liberalism by introducing alien and contradictory elements of socialism; and secondly, that he undermined the effective defence of liberalism by reason of his pacifism. If we are to form a just appraisal of Keynes's liberalism these matters must be dealt with squarely. In a certain sense, Keynes *did* introduce socialistic ideas, and he was committed to a certain form of pacifism. But he thought of both as an extension of liberalism, and I shall suggest that he was entitled so to think of them.

Let us take the theme of pacifism first. To what extent was Keynes a pacifist? He was clearly less of a pacifist than other members of the Bloomsbury Group; less of a pacifist, that is, than Lytton Strachey, Clive Bell or Roger Fry. He was less of a pacifist than such Cambridge friends as Lowes Dickinson and Bertrand Russell. But there is no doubt that his moral feelings during the First World War were closely akin to theirs. One of Bertrand Russell's several unkind remarks about Keynes was that Keynes was inwardly a pacifist but outwardly a government official during the First World War only because Keynes was too worldly and ambitious by nature to oppose the war publicly as Russell himself did. This is one example of the kind of uncharitable criticism to which Keynes was so often subject, especially from his friends.

If other pacifists saw Keynes as working for a 'war machine' in which he did not believe, he saw himself as using the privileged position that was offered him in the Civil Service in such a way as to try to moderate the folly and destructiveness of the war. It must surely be said that Bertrand Russell's aggressive antiwar activities, however courageous, and the scornful antipolitical attitudes of such Bloomsbury intellectuals as Lytton Strachey, however bold, were either totally ineffective, or even counterproductive from a pacifist point of view during the years between 1914 and 1918, though doubtless influential afterwards. But Keynes, byhis more discreet and subtle conduct, reached a point where in spite of his having registered in 1916 as a conscientious objector[1] he became a leading member of the British government's delegation to the peace conference which followed the armistice, as chief representative of the Treasury. Keynes was disappointed by the outcome of that conference, but at least he was able to judge it from the inside.

Keynes's pacifism has to be seen in the light of his general moral outlook, which he himself explains in his autobiographical writings[2] as something largely derived from the *Principia Ethica* of G. E. Moore, and shared by most other members of the Bloomsbury group: it was an intuitive as distinct from a utilitarian ethics, and particularly personal, almost aesthetic in character.

Unlike the out-and-out pacifist judgement that all war is wrong, Keynes felt that war in general is wrong, and that the 1914 war was not really an exception to that rule, as nearly all the Christians (on both sides) proclaimed. Even if there had been a case for England declaring war in August 1914, he felt that there was less and less a case for the way in which that war was continued stubbornly once the possibility of ending it had presented itself in 1915. When the French and British governments rejected the idea of negotiated peace in favour of victory at all costs, Keynes's pacifist feelings became increasingly intense; the wrongness of the war then being fought, and not just the wrongness of war in general, troubled him more acutely.

Of course Keynes was at odds then with what we think of as public opinion. Public opinion in 1914 was militaristic even jingoistic: most people expected a quick and exciting war. By 1918 this public opinion had changed; and a distinct revulsion against war became well-nigh universal. Those who had formerly been belligerent and imperialistic were disillusioned, embittered and often cynical. But Keynes was not of their number. He had no illusions to lose. He had never felt the thrill of war, only the evil of it. In February 1916 he had written to a tribunal for conscientious objectors: 'I do not say there are not conceivable circumstances in which I should voluntarily offer myself for military service. But having regard to the actually existing circumstances, I am certain it is not my duty to offer myself'.[3]

Keynes was a disappointed man after the peace conference in Paris in 1919; but his attitude was different from that emotional rejection of war which was to become so widespread in the 1920s and 1930s among people who had once been enthusiasts for war. The distinction is important, if only because Keynes is often accused of promoting that attitude. In fact, his was a reflective and deep-rooted pacifism, not the reaction of a man *bouleversé* by the horrors of war.

Keynes resigned from his post with the British delegation at the Paris peace conference in 1919 as a protest against the terms which the victorious Allies imposed on Germany, particularly in the matter of reparations and other economic penalties. The book which he wrote in these circumstances, *The Economic Consequences of the Peace*, is a masterpiece of political pamphleteering, combining powerful and clear arguments with brilliant literary style and imagery. Having always believed that the evils of war were tolerable, if tolerable at all, only if a just peace emerged at the end of it, Keynes now asserted forcefully that the Treaty of Versailles was an unjust peace. Moreover, he predicted that it was a settlement that would prove ruinous, not only for Germany, but for Europe as a whole.

*The Economic Consequences of the Peace* is a book too well known to stand in need of any detailed exposition: but briefly, Keynes maintained that both prudence and magnanimity should have dictated a peace settlement which would ensure the economic reconstruction of Europe. Europe, he explained, formed an economic system in which the industrial organisation of Germany was crucial to the wellbeing of the continent as a whole. He accused the Allied governments of refusing to accept these facts in their vindictive and shortsighted desire to make Germany 'pay for the war' by robbing her of most of her assets. Keynes further argued that the Peace of Versailles was an unjust peace, on the grounds that the Germans had surrendered on a clear understanding that Wilson's Fourteen Points would be the basis of the settlement, whereas in the event the Germans were forced to accept a peace which made a mockery of those Fourteen Points. For example, the right of all peoples to self-determination was one of the most important of Wilson's Fourteen Points, yet whenever the right of any German-speaking community to self-determination came into conflict with the expansionist aims of the Allies – in Sudetenland, Upper Silesia, East Prussia, the Saar, and so forth, that right was denied by the Treaty of Versailles to the German-speaking community.

Wilson's own avowed belief that the Treaty of Versailles was in accord with his Fourteen Points was seen by Keynes as evidence only of Wilson's obnoxious hypocrisy and self-deception. Among the famous short sketches of the leading statesmen at Paris in 1919 that Keynes provides in *The Economic Consequences of the Peace*, his characterisation of Woodrow Wilson is the most bitter and the most biting. Keynes demolished a popular idol with the same brisk wit that Lytton Strachey deployed afterwards in his *Eminent Victorians*. He is more polite towards Clemenceau, even though it was Clemenceau who forced the allies to accept a 'Carthaginian peace', as Keynes calls the Versailles settlement. Keynes could respect Clemenceau because Clemenceau was both intelligent and honest; Keynes notes that he was the only one of the four leading statesmen who could speak both French and English, that he was the only one who knew what he wanted and how to get it. He writes of Clemenceau, unforgettably, that 'he had one illusion, France, and one disillusion, mankind, including Frenchmen'.[4] Keynes does not reproach Clemenceau for his frank desire to intimidate and humiliate Germany without mercy; he blames the others, Orlando, Lloyd George and above all, Woodrow Wilson, for agreeing to do the same thing under the pretence that they were establishing democracy, freedom and economic reconstruction in Europe.

It may well be that Keynes, like all the best pamphleteers, forgot the virtue of charity in his zeal for justice, but if he was unkind to Wilson, he was surely right when he said that Wilson was at a loss in a world of practical politics, that Wilson could preach a sermon but neither think out nor put into effect a coherent political policy, and that Wilson had all the proverbial defects, as well as the temperament, of a provincial Nonconformist minister. All the biographical material concerning Wilson that has since come to light seems to me to confirm everything that Keynes says about him in *The Economic Consequences of the Peace*.

It is a book which attracted enormous attention when it was published in 1919; and in thinking about the influence of Keynes, the influence of this one book is something that calls for particular scrutiny. It is often said that this book did more harm than any other book published between the two wars. For example, at the first Keynes seminar, held at Canterbury in 1972, Roger Opie said:[5]

> It could be argued, I suppose, that Keynes caused the Second World War. That might be thought a slight exaggeration. And yet often in those interwar years, the Allied Powers might have acted to halt or at least frustrate Hitler's relentless drive to armed aggression. It was less a lack of power that made them hesitate and dither than a lack of moral confidence. . . There can be no doubt that Keynes's two books, *The Economic Consequences of the Peace* and *A Revision of the Treaty* were the most important factors in creating that intellectual, moral and political climate. The impact of the former book was, of course, enormous, it 'met with a reception which makes the word 'success' sound commonplace and insipid'.

Opie's remarks were doubtless intended as a paradox or joke; but even a joke must take account of the facts; and the crucial fact about the situation that Opie recalls is that by the time Hitler had emerged there were no longer 'Allied Powers' to act one way or the other; the USA had repudiated the alliance and withdrawn into neutrality; Italy had turned Fascist and was setting the example for Hitler to follow. England and France were on their own, and neither had sound reasons for trusting the other. The world of the 1930s, in short, was *not* the world of 1919; and what is more in the 1930s Keynes was saying things that were wholly appropriate to that altered world. If some readers refused to pay attention to his later writings and preferred to apply his earlier advice to a later situation, that was their folly and not his. The wording of Opie's remark is very characteristic of that used by critics of Keynes more serious in their hostility towards Keynes than Opie himself, who is, indeed, one of Keynes's most loyal admirers.

Among those critics who have said seriously what Opie said as a *plaisanterie*, is Etienne Mantoux, whose posthumous book *The Carthaginian Peace, or the Economic Consequences of Mr Keynes*[6] continues to affect people's judgement of Keynes – to affect and to distort it. Mantoux was a Frenchman who was partly educated in England, notably at the London School of Economics, where the impact of Harold Laski drove him, not unnaturally, rather far to the right. His book against Keynes is very Burkean in style and sentiment, and as a piece of pamphleteering it is as worthy to stand beside Keynes as Burke is worthy to stand beside Voltaire. Mantoux, as a young officer in the French Forces, died in an accident a few days before the end of the Second World War, but the book itself was actually written at a less exhilarating moment in French history – in 1942, in Princeton, where Mantoux had gone with a scholarship won in Vichy France in 1941. There is a certain grim bitterness about the book which matches the bitterness Keynes felt in 1919.

Mantoux's central argument is that Clemenceau was right; that the peace Clemenceau wanted was a just peace as well as a prudent peace, and that Wilson, Orlando and Lloyd George, in so far as they agreed with Clemenceau, acted wisely and well. Mantoux asserts that Keynes's charges of hypocrisy against Wilson are wholly unjustified, since the Treaty of Versailles established in Europe fair political frontiers and a tolerable economic order, all substantially in accord with Wilson's Fourteen Points. Mantoux denies that there was any immoderately punitive element towards Germany, and he accuses Keynes of gross exaggeration of the impoverishment and humiliation of Germany entailed by the terms of the Treaty.

Mantoux then goes on solemnly to make the charge that Opie made lightly, namely that Keynes by the influence of his writings propelled the world towards the Second World War. Mantoux suggests that Keynes's denigration of Woodrow Wilson had such an influence in America that it led the Americans to vote against Wilson and all that Wilson stood for – the League of Nations, the guarantees to France and all other commitments to Europe. According to Mantoux, Keynes was largely to blame for America turning its back in disgust on the Europe of the Versailles Treaty, and so depriving the new international structure of collective security of its most important element. Without American participation, the League of Nations was doomed from the start; and Mantoux holds Keynes responsible for having sabotaged that American participation.

Furthermore, Mantoux blames Keynes for having spread the idea that the Versailles Treaty was hypocritical and morally odious on the grounds that it violated the very principles of self-determination that it purported to sustain. At some length, and with great skill, Mantoux argues that there were sound economic reasons for placing under alien rule the Sudetenland, Upper Silesia, the Saar, the Polish Corridor and other places where there were German-speaking communities, and he repeats – as a mocking refrain – Keynes's own words that economic factors (iron, coal and transport) are more important than political frontiers for the wellbeing of Europe.

Thus Mantoux alleges that Keynes was responsible for propagating the notion, later exploited by Hitler, that the Versailles Treaty was so unjust that any effort by the Germans to overthrow or upset that Treaty would not only be tolerable, and forgivable, but might well be positively admirable.

Mantoux goes on to deny that the Treaty impoverished Germany economically to any serious extent, claiming that such economic amends as were demanded of Germany were ones that the Germans could well afford, as the subsequent recovery of Germany, and the massive rearmament of the Third Reich, amply demonstrated. He gives a good many statistics in support of this argument; but, as with Keynes himself in the *Economic Consequences*, it is the political reasoning, rather than the economic reasoning, which provides the real substance of the pamphlet. As a criticism of the policies adopted by France and England towards Germany in the years between 1919 and 1939, Mantoux's book is extremely persuasive; but as a criticism of Keynes, it is almost entirely off target.

It could fairly be said that Clemenceau was right in 1919 in the following sense: that the German people, being left under a unified and independent state, not only recovered quickly from the economic disabilities imposed by the peace settlement, but elected a fanatical dictator to lead them back to militarism and the reconquest of Europe, none of which could easily have happened if Germany had been broken up, like the Austrian Empire, into separate smaller states, deprived of heavy industries and occupied for a long period by Allied troops. In the event, of course, Clemenceau did not have his way. But neither did Keynes have his way. And it is perfectly reasonable to believe that the economic chaos in Germany which resulted from the Versailles settlement was largely responsible for the rise of Hitlerism. If the policy of economic reconstruction which Keynes recommended had been adopted then, constitutional government would have had as good a chance of success in Weimar Germany as it had after 1945 in the Bundesrepublik.

Furthermore, it needs to be emphasised that Keynes, after the rise of Hitler, no longer proposed a policy of reconciliation with the German government. He was one of the first and most unequivocal champions of resistance to the Nazi régime. Mantoux, very unfairly, quotes from Keynes's writings of 1919 and 1920 the word 'appeasement' and on the strength of this he declares that Keynes was the first exponent of appeasement. This is doubly unfair. Keynes used the word 'appeasement' in the context of a plea for reconciliation between the victorious nations of 1919 and the then new democratic German republic. The policy of appeasement of the Third Reich – and, of course, it was in that context that the word 'appeasement' became first notorious and then pejorative – was a policy put forward by Halifax and Chamberlain, and publicly opposed by Keynes.

I have mentioned Halifax, and it is instructive to recall that at the time of the Paris peace conference he, then Mr Wood, was strongly in favour of a harsh peace, and indeed it will be found that the most ardent militarists of 1919 were often the most anxious appeasers of 1938 and indeed the defeatists of 1940. It was not Keynes, but Lloyd George who prepared himself to enact the role of the British Petain in 1940; it was not Keynes, but Halifax who clung stubbornly at that time to the idea of a negotiated peace with the Third Reich. Mantoux says that the Keynesian policy of conciliation was at last put into practice in 1940 by Pierre Laval. But there is nothing 'Keynesian' whatever about Laval's conciliation of Hitler. Keynes had always opposed the conciliation of Hitler and advocated only the conciliation of another Germany, the democratic Germany which Hitler had destroyed.

The more we look at the things Keynes wrote after 1933 the more preposterous does the suggestion become that he was somehow to blame for the Second World War – rather the reverse. If what he had recommended at the time of Weimar had been adopted, there is every likelihood that Hitler would never have come to power; and if what Keynes recommended after 1933 had been adopted, the excesses of Hitler would have been resisted and thwarted sooner.

Keynes remained a pacifist in the sense that he continued to regard war as a great evil only to be tolerated in certain circumstances; but he believed that the circumstances were such that after 1933 the use of force against the Third Reich would be justified; that even a pacifist should fight Hitler. The spread of that idea can, I think, be fairly attributed to Keynes, but not the spread of appeasement or defeatism.

Of course, it is difficult to speak with confidence about the 'positive influence' of any theorist, but I think we might fairly see the influence of Keynes in the manner in which the Western powers approached the reconstruction of Europe after 1945. The German people were guiltier of far greater crimes in the Second World War than they were in the First World War, yet Churchill, De Gaulle and Truman, to their lasting credit, made peace in the manner of Keynes and not in the manner of Clemenceau. Germany and Italy after 1945 were restored economically, and Europe as a whole benefited, as Keynes had prophesied it would if the same policy had been adopted in 1919.

It is instructive to note that as early in the war as 1941,

Anthony Eden turned to Keynes for guidelines on the sort of 'order in Europe' that the Allies should seek to construct after a victorious end to the war. The proposals which Eden set forth on the basis of Keynes's advice were, broadly, the following:[7]

(a) close collaboration with the United States to institute a stable international economic order;
(b) international organisation of current arrangements and controls;
(c) international protection of free trade;
(d) the economic reconstruction of Germany, with any punitive measures confined to the military and political areas;
(e) a systematic relief and reconstruction programme for the whole of Europe.

These are all perhaps somewhat vague ideas, but Keynes himself was given enough authority by the wartime British government to see that some of them at least were translated into practice. The one unfortunate outcome was that the strain of the life of a statesman killed him at the age of 61. We ought not to deny him the credit for much that was meritorious in the peace that followed the Second World War.

* * *

When we turn from the theme of pacifism to that of socialism, we find Keynes subject to less articulate and systematic attacks. But nevertheless it is repeatedly said that Keynesian ideas propelled the free world on the road to socialism. And here perhaps it must be admitted that he exposed himself to such criticisms by the ambiguity of some of his utterances. We must however remember that throughout Keynes's lifetime, and even earlier, the leading philosophers of liberalism were destroying its traditional foundations by more radical transformations of liberal concepts than anything that Keynes himself proposed. If we consider the line of British liberal theorising that goes from J. S. Mill through T. H. Green to L. T. Hobhouse, we can see how the central liberal idea of liberty is first transformed from an idea of individual freedom into one of social freedom, and then transformed from social freedom into social justice. So that if we look at fairly recent studies of liberal thought, such as Lionel Trilling's *The Liberal Imagination* or Kenneth Minogue's *The Liberal Mind*, we find liberalism understood by the authors to be mainly a doctrine of social and economic betterment and hardly at all a doctrine of individual political rights.

I do not intend to go into the question as to whether this mutation of liberal philosophy had any connection with the decay of the Liberal Party of Great Britain, but it would hardly be surprising that once social radicalism is adopted as the main Liberal Party programme, people who care most for social change might prefer to vote for a Social Democratic or Labour Party, and people who yearn for the old ideal of individual freedom might prefer to vote for a moderate Conservative Party; in short, that a Liberal Party with a radical philosophy becomes unwanted both by the new devotees of social reform and the old adherents of individual liberty, so that at the level of practical politics, the British Liberal Party rendered itself superfluous, otiose, *de trop*, speeded on its way to electoral extinction by Mill, Green, Hobhouse and the other metaphysicians of British liberalism.

But Keynes stands apart from this endeavour to modernise liberalism by transforming its philosophy. What he tried deliberately, if sometimes deviously, to do, was to preserve the essential core of classical liberalism by attaching to it certain practical policies which he chose to call socialistic. Yet in doing this, Keynes seems to me to go straight back to the simple liberalism of Locke, and not in any way to subscribe to the idealistic and metaphysical philosophy of radical liberalism which emerged after J. S. Mill.

One of the most crucial arguments advanced by Keynes is that *laissez-faire* is *not* a sacred element of liberal political thought. Locke, after all, was not a *laissez-faire* theorist; he was very much a mercantilist, firmly believing that it was the duty of the government to act as guardian of the national economy. And Keynes, whose resemblances to Locke I have already emphasised, once again goes back to Lockeian principles – treating as an eighteenth-century innovation the idea of *laissez-faire* put forward by Adam Smith and David Hume.

Like Locke, Keynes believed that property must remain substantially in private hands if liberty is to prevail, but this did not seem to him to preclude the state overseeing the commercial and industrial activity of the nation. Keynes thought that such guidance (and the word 'planning' only came into his vocabulary in wartime when emergency measures were needed) could best be reconciled with private ownership by means of such semi-independent corporations as the Bank of England (an institution, which, incidentally, Locke had some share in founding). The sort of 'state control' Keynes envisaged was always organisational and not confiscatorial.

Naturally his proposals attracted the keenest public interest after 1929, when the world slump seemed to demonstrate the inadequacies of *laissez-faire* policies. His proposal for solving the problems of unemployment and recession by state spending, among other devices, found an eager public in America, and many believed (rightly or wrongly) that the New Deal owed some of its inspiration to Keynes.

But Keynes never advocated the nationalisation of the means of production. For example in his book of 1927, *Liberalism and Industry*, Keynes explains why he, as a liberal, rejects the Labour Party's proposals for state ownership. The Labour Party, he writes 'responds to anticommunist rubbish with anticapitalist rubbish'.[8] And elsewhere he wrote that for all his concern for social reform, 'the class war will find me on the side of the educated bourgeoisie'.[9] His contempt for Marxism was unmitigated: 'How can I adopt a creed which, preferring the mud to the fish, exalts the boorish proletariat above the bourgeois and intelligentsia who, with whatever faults, are the quality in life and carry the seeds of all human advancement.'[10]

We must not be misled by the word 'socialism' when Keynes chose to apply it from time to time to his own beliefs. For example, in a contribution to the *New Statesman* in 1939, Keynes wrote:

> The question is whether we are prepared to move out of the nineteenth-century *laissez-faire* state into the era of liberal socialism, by which I mean a system where we can act as an organised community for common purposes and to promote social and economic justice, whilst respecting and protecting the individual – his freedom of choice, his faith, his mind and its expression, his enterprise and his property'.[11]

I myself feel that Keynes would have done better to speak of his credo as social-liberalism rather than liberal-socialism, for an avowal of socialism, albeit liberal, seems only to confirm Hayek's suggestion that Keynesian proposals necessarily entail a sacrifice of the individual to the state. Alternatively, it might be suggested that Keynes in 1939 was already thinking in terms of a wartime economy.

That there is such a thing as liberal-socialism, we need not doubt: Gaitskell and Jenkins may be numbered among its noted exponents. But Keynes is not really of their number. It is true that as early as 1924 Keynes had professed himself a champion of 'true socialism',[12] but we all know that anyone who claims to believe in true anything – true religion, true chastity, true fidelity or whatever – really means the opposite. 'True temperance', says a character in one of Aldous Huxley's novels, 'is half a bottle of claret with every meal and three double whiskies after dinner'. We can confidently assume that anyone who believes in true socialism does not believe in socialism at all.

Moreover in talking about Keynes's liberalism or Keynes's socialism we have always to keep in mind what Seymour Harris calls Keynes's 'dislike and distrust of politicians'.[13] Although Keynes went into Parliament as a member of the House of Lords in 1942 and took part in debates there from time to time, he had much less faith in parliamentary politics than Locke had, even though Locke never went into parliament. Keynes really belonged with Francis Bacon, and the *philosophes*, and the utilitarians and the Fabians, to that class of intellectual which believes that intellectuals should rule. He did not think that political debates would come up with the right answer to the nation's problems. Those problems should be solved in their heads by men with good enough brains to work out rational solutions to them.

The self-styled 'Keynesian' politician is a paradoxical figure, in the sense that Keynesianism implied the diminution of the politician and the elevation of the administrator. The British tradition of parliamentary rule, aided by a fairly amateurish civil service, is alien to the Keynesian scheme of things. It is in France, and to a lesser extent in America, that Keynesian ideas have been best understood. It is in the Fifth Republic, where what De Gaulle contemptuously called 'the politicians and the parties' have been humbled, and a highly trained *élite* of administrators given great opportunities and powers, where the mixed economy has been built on the basis of free enterprise rather than nationalisation, where the trade unions have less than half the strength they have in England, that Keynesian proposals have had their fullest embodiment in action so far. There are many of Keynes's ideas in Giscard d'Estaing's recent pamphlet *La Democracie Française* – not as well expressed as Keynes himself would have expressed them, but all manifestly his. Indeed the presidential system of government, whether French or American, offers more scope for enlightened management of the economy than does the British parliamentary system, and it is that much easier for a Giscard, or a Carter, to put Keynesian ideas into practice than it is for his own countrymen, however highly placed.

When the British Empire was still in being, large parts of it were, in effect, governed by a superior class of administrators. Keynes began his own career in 1906 in the India Office as a member of one such *élite*, and this experience shaped his attitude to politics for the rest of his life.

Schumpeter once said of Keynes that 'like the old free traders, he always exalted what was at any moment truth and wisdom for England into truth and wisdom for all times and places'.[14] But Schumpeter is wrong. Keynes, like Locke, dealt with political ideas at a high level of abstraction so that readers all over the world were able to recognise the relevance of the author's suggestions to their own problems. It is indeed arguable that of all peoples, the English have understood Keynes least, and profited least from what he had to offer.

Two of Keynes's most important critics – von Hayek and von Mises – held that Keynes's mixture of liberty and state guidance simply will not work, that you have to settle for the one or the other. The experience of several countries suggests that Keynes was right; that his mixture does work. It is unfortunate that Great Britain is not one of them. We have rejected *laissez-faire*, as he wished, but we have adopted what he did not wish – nationalisation, a punitive taxation, an ignorant bureaucracy, and trade union despotism, a lavish pursuit of egalitarianism and an antibourgeois ideology. We have cultivated all those features of socialism which he most detested. It is ironical that he should be blamed for this melancholy situation.

I suggested in the first part of this paper that the kind of appeasement we witnessed in the 1930s was not at all the kind of appeasement Keynes advocated in 1919. I would add that the kind of mixed economy we have in Great Britain in the 1970s is not at all the mixed economy Keynes recommended in the numerous writings he published in the 1930s and 1940s. Anyone who thinks, in either case, that Keynes was the 'inspiration', cannot have read what Keynes actually wrote.

NOTES

1. See D. E. Moggridge, *Keynes* (1976), p. 16.
2. See especially 'My Early Beliefs' in the *Collected Writings*, Vol. X, pp. 435–47.
3. Moggridge, op. cit., p. 18.
4. *The Economic Consequences of the Peace* (London: 1919), p. 29.
5. In D. E. Moggridge (ed.) *Keynes: Aspects of the Man and His Work* (London: 1974), p. 74.
6. (London: 1945). Published in French as *La Paix Calomniée* (Paris: 1946), but actually written in English by Mantoux himself.
7. For details see Moggridge, op. cit., pp. 138–41.
8. *Liberalism and Industry* (London: 1927), p. 206.
9. Quoted by Seymour Harris, *Keynes* (New York: 1955), p. 76.
10. *Essays in Persuasion* (London: 1931), p. 300.
11. Quoted by Moggridge, op. cit., pp. 44–5.
12. Harris, op. cit., p. 73.
13. Ibid., p. 79.
14. Quoted by Harris, op. cit., pp. 211–12.

## DISCUSSION

*Mr Hoffman:* Professor Cranston mentioned that Keynes was an active opposer of appeasement in 1939. During the 1930s did he in fact say anything about rearmament, or did he not come out with anything firm on the subject at all?

*Professor Cranston:* We can see from Keynes's own publications that he favoured armed resistance to Hitler at a time when other people – Kingsley Martin for example – were trying to be at the same time pacificists and antifascists. Martin's whole attitude to war was equivocal; and in this he was not unique. But Keynes was very clearcut in his attitude to international affairs throughout the 1930s, and I could give you chapter and verse to justify that view. He recognised that pacificism and opposition to Hitler were incompatible, and that pacificism would have to be set aside.

*Mr Opie:* Rather than ask a question could I just make a couple of very short comments on both of the preceding papers? Professor Cranston quoted from my paper at the first Keynes Seminar in 1972 and he suggested that perhaps what I said – namely that Keynes might have caused the Second World War – was said as a joke. It underlines the importance of the difference between the spoken word and the written word. It wasn't a joke so much as a deliberate provocation. I'm reminded of a phrase used by the hero of a recent series of television plays about Cambridge – *The Glittering Prizes* – in which the young man said 'words are loaded pistols'. It is clear that one has to be very careful in which direction the pistol is pointing. So I confirm what Professor Cranston said. It was partly meant as a joke, or at least a deliberate provocation of an audience.

The other comment I would like to make is on what Dr Skidelsky has said. He was talking about the influence of the advisers on President Kennedy. As I understand it, in a curious sort of way, what was called the new economics in the Kennedy period was almost a total triumph of conservatism. President Kennedy was very eager not to be thought a profligate democratic spender, and Walter Heller, who was chairman of the

Council of Economic Advisers, was brilliantly successful in persuading Kennedy that the only way to balance the budget and to outsmart the Republicans was actually to cut taxes. Now that is a very super-sophisticated use of the Kahn multiplier and it worked. That of course may well be exactly the situation now.

This brings me to my second comment. In this country, where we are terrified of the public sector borrowing requirement, one of the lines which is now being propounded is that the one way to eliminate so-called inflationary government spending is to return to full employment when we shall be back in balance. So one wonders whether all the arguments during the 1930s that you cannot spend your way out of a slump are not now coming around full circle, where businessmen, I'm told, believe that indeed you can no longer spend your way out of a slump. On the contrary – as I'm told was the view in Roosevelt's day – businessmen think of public spending as being not complementary, and not indeed (as I think Dr Skidelsky was suggesting) as the basis of their profits, but rather as competitive. One of my memories of the criticism of Keynesian/Rooseveltian policies in the thirties was the bitter opposition to the Tennessee Valley Authority, which no doubt was expansionary in its expenditure effects, but the opposition saw it as strictly competitive. It wiped out rather than created possibilities of profit. Now here we are back in the 1970s, 40 years after the *General Theory*, and we have exactly the same view expressed, that is to say public spending far from being complementary to private prosperity is actually competitive with it, and unless we cut the one we cannot have more of the other. I just wonder whether Dr Skidelsky has any comment on this curious paradox that we seem to have come full circle and have turned our backs entirely on what seems to me to be an elementary truth.

*Dr Skidelsky:* On the Tennessee Valley Authority, I'm not sure it was the spending as much as the institutional structures that were set up that aroused business hostility. There was a mixture of recovery and reform in so many of the things that Roosevelt was toying with and one really has to ask what bits people were actually objecting to. My impression from what I read and from a number of accounts of this period does suggest that their hostility was not directed so much to the spending programmes; that there was a lot of support for spending programmes especially early on in the whole thing, but that support was lost for the New Deal by all the other elements in which the New Dealers were interested. I'll think about what you said about the contemporary implications of this.

*Dr Dean:* I wonder whether Dr Skidelsky will comment on what I think is the essential point about the New Deal and that is that almost all New Dealers were anxious above everything else to increase the purchasing power of the masses. This seems to me, therefore, almost to prejudge redistribution of income and things of that kind. Do you think that is right?

*Dr Skidelsky:* I think they were eager to do what you say but they were trying to do it in a curious way by institutional changes; for example, acting against monopolies who were holding up prices instead of allowing them to fall and that kind of thing. I entirely agree with what you say that there was a general eagerness to increase mass purchasing power in line with an underconsumptionist analysis of the Depression which was quite prevalent, but it went with an attempt to change institutions in order to achieve the increase in purchasing power. And really what Keynes was saying was that you can do this without institutional change. I don't think the New Dealers were prepared to abandon their reformist aims until they had tried everything or were given the political strength to do the various things they were trying to do, and that came right at the end of the thirties.

*Anonymous:* I would like to address a question to Dr Skidelsky. He has given us a fascinating account of the advent of Keynesianism in the United States and its acceptance as a basis of American policy by about the time that President Kennedy came into office. My question to him is: could he carry the story on beyond that, because the developments since 1964 have, of course, been very striking indeed? One saw the development of deficit financing originating from two main sources: the growth of spending on the Vietnam war, and the development of social policies as exemplified by the Johnson great society. The effect of these two policies – to mention no others – was to produce the emergence of very strong inflationary developments in the United States. You will recall also that this was the period of the emergence of the chronic United States balance of payments deficit and all that this implied in the shape of the growth of external reserves of other countries that were helping to finance the deficit and so on. I would very much like to hear, and I'm sure others would too, how Dr Skidelsky would evaluate the development of Keynesian thought and its impact on policy in the years since 1964.

*Dr Skidelsky:* I'm not very competent to say much about this. One of the things that I was really struck by when looking at this whole subject was the extraordinary lack of any kind of empirical support for some of the main Keynesian postulates. For example, Professor Stein in his book *The Fiscal Revolution*, which I think is the most detailed account of the coming of Keynesianism to America, says that there is no correlation between movements of the budget and movements of the economy in successive periods since 1945 that has been convincingly established at all, not even as to direction. Now that was written in 1969 and I just don't know what the situation has been since then and what has caused the inflation. I think we really don't know and this is why economics is in such a ferment today, in Britain as well as in America.

*Dr Nabiel:* It seems to me that there is some confusion about what is and what is not Keynesian policy.

First of all, about the New Deal. I do not accept that the New Deal can be considered as a type of Keynesian policy if by this we understand a certain governmental strategy in managing the economy. The New Deal was not seen as such an instrument but rather as an enlarged programme of public works intended to alleviate the burden of unemployment in expectation of the recovery which was considered to come in the normal course of events. If we look at the criticism which at the time was directed against the New Deal by its opponents, it was not from the position of overall economic policy but rather on the grounds that essentially it was ineffective and that to a large extent it was competing with private enterprise and private investment, and therefore by increasing employment in one sector it reduced employment in another.

Kahn's multiplier was at the time a theoretical formula discussed among academics but was far from being accepted as a guideline for policy. I would not, therefore, link the New Deal too much with Keynesian policy as such.

If we now turn to the post-Second World War period I do not think that it is right to link the effectiveness or ineffectiveness of economic policy in the United States with the extent to which various governments pursued Keynesian remedies. The essence of Keynesianism is the acceptance of the state's responsibility for managing the economy, and, more specifically, managing aggregate demand, maintaining full employment, price stability and a desired rate of growth. This is essentially what the contemporary understanding of Keynesianism is about, but Keynes did not provide a recipe on how to manage the economy and this cannot be done anyway as there is not just one recipe.

The *General Theory* contained a fundamental economic ideology but not a practical guideline for implementation. The latter is a continuous process which, particularly in the light of recent experience of the so-called tradeoff between inflation and unemployment, needs a lot of rethinking and reassessment. Whether policies pursued by governments in the United States are effective or ineffective neither proves nor disproves Keynes's central message.

The second point I would like to make concerns Dr Skidelsky's proposition that both main political parties in the United States accepted the Keynesian remedies. It seems to me that there is a degree of oversimplification in overlooking the important difference between the two parties. While the Democratic Party essentially accepted the principle of government responsibility for managing the economy, the Republican Party in all its election campaigns took the opposite view proclaiming the traditional belief in free enterprise, the unhindered operation of market forces, and minimum state interference in economic life. It is true that when the Republicans came to power, and this applies both to the Eisenhower and to the Nixon period, their practical policies were not very consistent with their electoral manifestos and that, in practice, they found it necessary to pursue an interventionist economic policy.

Finally, I think that in the analysis of the American response to Keynes it is worth noting the important difference between what was the Keynesian response in the United States on the one hand and in Western Europe on the other. While in Western Europe the acceptance of a mixed economy and of a public sector has been largely part of this response, in the United States this has not been the case, and even among the more orthodox protagonists of Keynesian policies the proposition of expanding the public sector and moving towards a mixed economy did not have strong adherence.

*Dr Skidelsky:* I have no disagreement with what the speaker says.

*Mr Daines:* I was rather confused, Professor Cranston, by your discussion of liberalism. At one stage you seemed to be saying that Keynes was going back to a pre-Adam Smith concern, not worried about *laissez-faire* in the same sense that Smith and later liberals were worried about *laissez-faire*; yet on the other hand you seemed to be saying that he was rejecting T. H. Green and Hobhouse and other people who were concerned with social liberalism and who also rejected *laissez-faire*. It may be just my confusion, but could you clarify?

*Professor Cranston:* Certainly I'll try to do so. What I had in mind was that Keynes's liberalism was really based on two propositions. First the supreme value of liberty, and secondly the belief that private property was a necessary condition for liberty to be experienced. By liberty he meant the liberty of each individual person. He was not influenced by the sort of Oxford type of liberalism which is very much embodied in T. H. Green, who thinks that liberty is some kind of shared experience of society as a whole. Therefore in his notion of what liberty was he goes back to the seventeenth and eighteenth century. But he does not accept the innovations of Adam Smith – the idea of *laissez-faire* being some kind of dogma. He is quite happy to go back to Locke's idea that the state has a very important role to play in a free society, notably a role to play in supervising the management of the economy. For example, the institution of the Board of Trade and the Bank of England, which were very important to Locke's point of view, seem to me to be just the kind of thing which Keynes would have thought a liberal state should be doing, and this is quite distinct from social measures such as setting up comprehensive schools or setting up nationalised steelworks and that kind of thing, which twentieth-century opinion seems to favour. But I introduced the name of Green because so many of the critics of Keynes seem to think that Keynes came along when liberal opinion was completely committed to *laissez-faire* doctrines and individualism and directed it towards socialistic views. This seems to me to be not the case. Long before Keynes started to work, liberal opinion was moving towards notions of society, the notion of social improvement and using the state to introduce equality. Keynes was not in this sense the man who introduced the social notion. In fact I think that Keynes had very much less of a social notion than most liberal members of the House of Commons had in 1912.

*Professor Vile:* Could I use my position as chairman to ask both speakers two questions which seem to me to be very important? Firstly I would be interested to know whether Dr Skidelsky in presenting Keynes's influence in the United States as one which was almost irrelevant to what happened, in the sense that people merely adopted his ideas as a convenient vehicle for what they wanted to do anyway, is using this as an example of a kind of world view of what political or economic thinkers can or cannot achieve. On this question there seemed to me a considerable difference between Dr Skidelsky and Professor Cranston, in the sense that Dr Skidelsky seemed to be saying that really the ideas of Keynes had no direct effect in themselves, they were just used by businessmen and politicians to pursue their aims, whereas Professor Cranston was giving serious consideration to such ideas as that Keynes started the Second World War. These are totally different views of the impact a political thinker might have.

My second point about the impact of Keynes on political economic thought is that the one thing that one can surely point to as Keynes's really clear effect upon modern society is that above all he made respectable a high level of government spending, not in a socialist economy or a communist state, but in a liberal-mixed–social-democratic context. It is this – quite apart from whether he was successful in terms of his ability to suggest ways in which to control the economy – which has really transformed the economic situation and which I think is the reason why we have got back, as Mr Opie says, to seeing private and public expenditure as competitive rather than as things which are complementary. This is the really fundamental impact of Keynes upon the modern world: to make the mixed economy respectable.

*Dr Skidelsky:* I didn't of course want to imply that ideas have no power of their own. That would be absurd. But what I was trying to ask was the question of why are some ideas taken up rather than others? I suppose one could ask that about two different groups of people. Why they are taken up by economists; why they are taken up by the users of ideas: politicians? I find the question both fascinating and very, very complex. I was really suggesting here that when you ask why did economists become converted to Keynesian ideas you have to give purely intellectual, logical reasons relating to the theory being put forward, but I also tried to use a bit of sociology of knowledge and said that Keynesian theories were good for the status of economists. They have proved to be good for the status of economists, and this may have been one of the reasons why they were accorded a warm welcome, especially among younger economists in the thirties. When you ask why politicians take up the Keynesian route to recovery from depression, rather than some other route, the answer becomes very complicated. There were other ways of solving unemployment in the thirties. Hitler solved unemployment without ever using Keynes. In fact I think Joan Robinson once wrote somewhere that Hitler had cured unemployment before Keynes had even started explaining why it occurred. So there were different ways of doing it, and why you did it by the Keynesian route rather than by some other route was presumably partly because of other values you held, for example not wanting to interfere with liberty, or not wanting to take over industry, and partly also because politically it was easier to do it that way than by some other route. I do find the problem difficult, but I didn't want to give the impression that I was being Machiavellian about this and thinking that ideas are purely instrumental. I was just trying to redress the balance of what seemed to me the conventional accounts of the reception of Keynesianism into America.

*Professor Cranston:* Perhaps I might go on to draw an analogy between Keynes and Locke. You see I think people as distinguished and distinctive and special as they were have at least two personalities. There is the actual author and the actual text which has a certain impact on the close readers; and then they also inject into the culture some body of thought and feeling. Now if you look at the eighteenth century it might be asked what is the actual influence of Locke on the American Revolution and all the things that happened in the United States? Well, you might begin by asking did Jefferson read Locke? Did Hamilton read Locke? Do Jefferson's publications reflect a sort of Lockeian language, and so on? One could argue for many, many years about that sort of question. Then you might ask a different sort of question. How Lockeian, in a rather general sense, did a certain approach to politics, a very important approach to politics, express itself in the eighteenth century?

Now the same sorts of questions can be asked of Keynes in the twentieth century; although the actual areas of Locke and Keynes are rather different – they both did these two important things. They enriched, as it were, the philosophy, and the highest theoretical analysis in which scholars engage, and they also gave something to the world which people who are not experts in their field have appreciated. The unfortunate thing, I think, in the case of Keynes, however, is that the world hasn't got it quite right. There is a sort of distorted Keynes, as well as a correct Keynes, which has penetrated the culture. Therefore there is a duty on those who think about these things carefully to try and correct the 'public' Keynes or the message or the teaching of the 'public' Keynes which is not so necessary with the 'public' Locke. That is really what I am trying to say.

*Sir Austin Robinson:* I wonder whether I might go back for one moment to something that Dr Skidelsky was saying just now. It worries me to assume that the Harvard economists who embraced Keynesian theories did so because this was the profitable, careerist thing to do. These are people I knew extremely well, and I don't believe it was quite as simple as that. Because what I find awfully odd is that out of Dr Skidelsky's very convincing story one thing seems to have got left out and that is the fact that the world was going through a major crisis at that time, and that those of us who were living with this crisis, rather like some of our contemporaries today, really minded about the state of employment and really wanted to do something about it. The people I knew best, Lauchlan Currie, Walter Salant, Kenneth Galbraith and the rest, minded about that state of the world. It may have helped their careers slightly that they embraced Keynesian theories, but I think that they were much more concerned in trying to do something about the world than with trying to find a theory that would get them into a profitable job in Washington.

*Dr Skidelsky:* With great respect to Sir Austin Robinson, he has simply taken one bit of an explanation I gave and said that that is the whole thing. I, of course, never either said or implied that the reason that economists took up Keynesian ideas was because they saw it would help their careers either individually or collectively. Also to say that the various people Sir Austin Robinson mentioned were interested or wanted to help in a very grave situation is perfectly true, but that doesn't distinguish them from any other people who also felt very concerned and very helpless in the face of these calamities and wanted to do something about them. No, what I was saying was that the impact of ideas on a profession has to be explained in a number of different ways, and it always does, and that is a basic principle of explanation that an historian has to use. You have to try and combine different elements: the power and appeal of the ideas themselves, the perception of their utility in solving particular problems, and their impact also on the profession. I think all these things have to be borne in mind. I certainly don't want to imply that those people you mention adopted Keynes because they thought it would give them cushy government jobs.

*Mr Carr:* I would like to suggest that the fact that deficit spending as a way out of unemployment appears to be out of fashion in some places, doesn't imply that the Keynesian analysis is being rejected by modern governments and their advisers. It is rather a learning process and a realisation that the world is rather more complicated than the simplest so-called Keynesian economic models imply. I would like just to instance the thinking of the French government exemplified in the model that underlies their economic plan. Since 1962 it has been the normal practice in France to aim at balancing the budget in normal circumstances. The theory behind this is that you can divide the economy into a trading sector and a non-trading sector, and the trading sector is part of an open-world economy and employment depends on the competitiveness of the trading sector rather than on the level of government spending and the size of the deficit. And some kind of match between saving and investment in the public sector is achieved by financing most public sector borrowing of local authorities and nationalised industries through the national savings banks which can mobilise and lend the funds that are deposited by savers in the national savings banks, and that amount is available to be lent to approved borrowers mainly in the public sector. I think this is a sort of refinement of Keynesianism. But the underlying possibility of a world recession is certainly accepted and in fact the French budget was deliberately unbalanced in 1975 as a response to the world recession. But what the French government does not believe is that France can spend itself out of a recession just by increasing expenditure in the public sector – the non-trading sector – in the open economy in which it now exists.

# Concluding Remarks

*R. G. Jones* (Deputy Master of Keynes College)

My understanding of economics goes no further than the tales of doom and impending disaster that I read in the daily newspapers and the letters I receive from my bank manager. Nevertheless, I must say that I've always found these seminars very interesting. However, with the British economy currently sliding downhill, I hope you will indulge me, if, as a natural scientist, I make one observation. I feel that social scientists, amongst scientists, start from a disadvantageous position. As Professor Corry said, 'social scientists must convince each other theoretically'. Natural scientists on the other hand have the added advantage of being able to construct real physical models of what they wish to achieve. As a consequence, perhaps, we seem to get into trouble of a lesser magnitude than do social scientists. Forgive me for making this observation but I think it is relevant to our present situation in which it seems that on every occasion that Mr Healey stands up in the House of Commons, we hear of yet another economic crisis on a scale akin to that of the Flixborough disaster. If only it were possible for social scientists to construct pilot plants on which they could test their ideas before implementing them!

My main job at the moment, however, is to thank our distinguished speakers for giving us an interesting and stimulating afternoon. I should also like to thank Mr Farmiloe and Macmillan, the publishers of the seminar proceedings, for their continued interest, and I trust that everybody will join me in expressing their appreciation in the usual way.

# Index